GANGSTERNOMICS ™

BY

JOHN SUROWY

BOOKING INFORMATION

To book the author of GangsterNomics for a media appearance, speaking engagement or corporate event contact us at:

BOOKING@GANGSTERNOMICS.COM

This book is dedicated to my beloved family.

TABLE OF CONTENTS

11

"The Best Crimes Are Completely Legal"

- Old GangsterNomics Proverb

ALL BUSINESS IS WAR

All business is war, and all war is business. That is the philosophy of an unholy alliance of gangsters, cartels and corporations now economically conspiring to take your job, home, company and savings with a ruthless and diabolically clever new set of business models. GangsterNomics reveals their secrets, and provides you with the information you'll need to survive and prosper during their next wave of silent economic attacks.

This alliance is unique in that they're united only by the similarity of their business models and commonality of their goal, which is to transfer as much of your wealth into their hands as quickly as possible.

GangsterNomics reveals their very successful business models, and then describes how you can use a modified version of those models to enhance your own legitimate business endeavors. This is crucial because, while business has always possessed similarities to war, it is now becoming so ruthless and Machiavellian that in many ways it's worse. If you think this is an exaggeration then read the story that follows, and keep in mind that most wars would never permit the level of violence you're about to see described.

Mobster Dutch Shultz and his gang once performed a cost versus benefit analysis. The gang decided they would dramatically increase their revenues if they could start providing beer to some of their rivals, so they began by allegedly kidnapping a bar owner named Joe Rock. Joe wasn't just tough, he was legendary. Unfortunately for him the Shultz gang was determined to grow their business, and they wouldn't take no for an answer. They wanted to expand, and that meant forcing guys like Joe to buy beer from them. So what did they do? They allegedly suspended Joe from a meat hook and then taped a gauze bandage onto his eyes that was soaked with the discharge from a gonorrhea infection. Joe's family reportedly turned over $35,000 to get him released, but shortly after that Joe went blind anyway. Needless to say, the Shultz gang went on to dominate beer distribution.

Think this medieval behavior doesn't continue in today's modern business world? Not only does it continue, but it has become much worse.

The Dutch Shultz situation is a very early example of highly aggressive market share acquisition. If you've always wondered why gangsters, dictators, drug dealers and crooked CEOs always seem to make money no matter how difficult the economy is, then read on.

Forget the nonsense they taught you in business school. Most business professors wouldn't be working there if they had any ability to make serious money elsewhere.

Forget the advice your CPA is giving you. Great fortunes are never amassed by playing it safe, and CPAs are the very definition of financial conservatism.

Forget everything you've done up until now. If what you were doing up until this point was getting serious results, then you'd be lying on a Brazilian beach somewhere, sipping margaritas and counting your cash.

You're reading this book because deep down inside, your instincts are telling you something is very wrong out there. You sense that if you don't do something dramatic soon, you'll regret it. If there is any doubt in your mind, walk down the aisles of any major discount store these days and take a look at the startling number of senior citizens who work there for near minimum wage. Almost every one of those people started out their lives with big dreams, great ambitions, and a strong work ethic. Now look at them....

WHAT IS GANGSTERNOMICS

We are now moving into an era where the ethical behavior of major corporations and financial institutions bears a growing similarity to the behavior of some of history's greatest gangsters, dictators and thugs.

GangsterNomics is the study of the business practices of some of the world's most notorious and successful gangsters, corrupt CEOs and drug dealers. We will then show you how to apply those same techniques and ruthless business models to your own career, investment portfolio and business practices. Simply put, we are going to show you how the ruthlessly wealthy always seem to get wealthier.

Why would you want to know that? Because gangsters have many things in common, and one of them is an unerring ability to succeed in business. The average person will instantly assume that gangsters succeed because of intimidation and violence, but the truth of the matter is that, statistically speaking, violence is rarely used by gangsters. What they do use very effectively is a set of rules and policies which, when viewed from a business prospective, bear a very striking resemblance to hyper-aggressive business models.

In GangsterNomics, we will distill many of their practices down to something that can be applied to your economic life, career and business beliefs.

So without any further adieu, pull down the shades, bolt the door and put on a bulletproof vest, because everything you thought you knew about business is going to change. Welcome to GangsterNomics.

SOCIOPATHIC BUSINESS MODELS

In the business world, the current movement is away from the Judaic Christian ethic and towards a GangsterNomic business mindset, which can best be described as sociopathic. While conventional business behavior was once governed by a belief that limited one's actions whenever there was a possibility it might cause ill will or a moral backlash, today those objections would be viewed as dated and unrealistic.

The business behavior of most criminals and corporations is now governed by only two criteria. Will this business generate a profit, and will it result in governmental intervention of some sort? If it is deemed to be profitable enough to outweigh the consequences of governmental intervention, then most will decide to proceed. Ultimately, they will view the problems it causes as simply a cost of conducting this particular business.

What's interesting is that the same tactics are being employed by both organized crime and the corporate world. Each will pour tremendous time and energy into creating the impression that their businesses are well-intentioned and morally correct. In reality, those things have little or nothing to do with their real goal, which is to generate as much profit as possible before the opportunity fades or the government intervenes.

Sociopathic business models typically involve activities that were once considered illegal or immoral, but have now been legislated into the very mainstream of commerce.

We are not just talking about gambling or prostitution, but the manner in which ruthless activity has been mainstreamed into every aspect of commercial behavior. Rather than being shamed back into the shadows, ruthless behavior has now been elevated to celebrity status in sports, business and most other aspects of modern culture.

You can usually identify a sociopathic business model by the way it makes people feel uncomfortable. It's not because the practices are illegal (they almost never are), but because these models just make it seem like they are exploiting people (they usually are).

WHAT IS A GANGSTER

A gangster is just a sociopathic entrepreneur who's willing to push the envelope further than most. In fact, the only thing that separates most gangsters from most CEOs is the degree to which they're willing to push that envelope.

Put most gangsters in a room with most CEOs and you'll find that two things occur. The first is that they instinctively distrust each other, because they see so much of themselves in the other guy. The second thing that happens is that they tend to get along pretty well, because they're both pretty charming and likable. They probably won't spend time together at the golf course, but it wouldn't be hard to coax either of them into an evening at the strip club.

The difference between gangsters, CEOs and the rest of us is that most of us are at the club to enjoy the view. When gangsters and CEOs go to a club, they're calculating how much money the owner is making off the club, and how one might open a better bar. Gangsters evaluate, look for weaknesses and then try and take control, just like CEOs do in the marketplace. Whereas the rest of society simply becomes part of their environment, gangsters see the environment as something they can control and influence for profit's sake.

FOURTEEN SIGNS OF A PENDING
ECONOMIC COLLAPSE

Before we move on to the next stage of this book, it's important for you to understand GangsterNomics and how our economy is fostering its growth. GangsterNomics is the result of economic adversity. In fact, that's what fuels its growth. The harder things get, the more gangster they get. Here are some signs that the economy is about to get more GangsterNomic than it has ever been before:

1) Pension funds are being downsized or eliminated. This is already beginning at many major companies, and it's a dam that will continue to break. It is a very bad sign, and a classic GangsterNomic indication that all other options have been exhausted or compromised.

2) Homes that used to sell in ten days now take ten months. This phenomenon first began to occur in many high-end homes, and has now become increasingly common in the mid-price range. It is largely a function of job losses.

3) Property tax payments are now beginning to equal monthly mortgage payments in some cities.

4) An increasing number of federal agencies and local municipalities are admitting they cannot provide an accurate accounting statement for some of their departments. This is often the lie of last resort that occurs when an economic reckoning appears to be inevitable. The accounting books and computer files are whitewashed to conceal all the theft and mismanagement that has occurred over time. It usually means that the robbing and stealing has become so outrageous, there's no reasonable way to hide it. You've just got to trash everything, and blame the computers or the bookkeepers.

5) The number of bankruptcies is accelerating at a phenomenal rate. In 2005, the government passed the

Bankruptcy Abuse Prevention and Consumer Protection Act, which is designed to make it extremely difficult for people saddled with credit card debt to ever rid themselves of it. In some major U.S. cities with more than one casino, the bankruptcy rate has climbed so fast that attorneys now openly joke about wishing they could open a combination bankruptcy law firm/hot dog stand at the front and rear entrances of each casino.

6) Temporary employment agencies now hire more people than many Fortune 500 firms. If you think that's bad, then you'll love this: some computer companies are now flying in planeloads of programmers from Asia. They put them up in a hotel for a month or two, have them work on major projects, and then fly them back home again. Even with all the transportation and lodging expenses, it's still much cheaper than hiring domestic programmers.

7) Mortgage companies have begun offering forty-year mortgages. For many people this means they will not pay their mortgage off in their lifetimes. In Japan the average mortgage term is 100 years, which means that families pass mortgages down from generation to generation.

8) For a growing number of vehicles, the monthly cost of purchasing gas and insurance is now equal to or greater than the monthly car payment.

9) Before hiring you for a near-minimum wage job, many companies will now have you fill out an application that contains questions designed to assess your psychological makeup, have you submit to a urine screen for drugs, and best of all, they will run your credit report to see what kind of financial shape you're in. A red flag in any of these areas can instantly disqualify you from being hired as a toilet paper salesman in aisle six of your friendly neighborhood retailer. No city in the United States requires its mayoral candidates to submit to psychological exams, drug tests or credit checks before running for mayor, yet

companies routinely demand this of people applying for the lowest paying jobs.

10) You will begin to see a dramatic rise in multi-generational family cohabitation. Grandparents, parents, children and grandchildren will begin living together under one roof, out of economic necessity.

11) A rapid rise in the sale of interest-only mortgages. These allow you to buy a home with a smaller monthly payment because all you are doing is paying the interest on the mortgage without ever really paying down the principal. This is very significant, because most homeowners think that their home will appreciate over time and provide them with some equity. The irony is that, if you talk to a real estate expert behind closed doors and he trusts you, he will tell you that the real estate bubble is already beginning to pop. When this baby blows you are going to see an economic meltdown like no other. Most people will be living in homes that are worth less than they paid for them. Homeowners who purchase interest-only mortgages will have the added distinction of living in homes that are worth less than the original purchase price, and that have a principal on the mortgage balance that won't go down a single penny over the next thirty years.

12) A massive deployment of American jobs offshore. Jobs at every level of the economy, from seamstresses to radiologists, are now being sent overseas at such an accelerating rate that the probability of this phenomenon slowing down or being reversed in the near future appears highly unlikely.

13) In 2005, the United States Supreme Court widened the scope of property seizure laws. They ruled that the Fifth Amendment's Takings Clause permits government seizure of private property for commercial gain. In layman's terms, this means that if a developer decides he can make money with your property, then he can have the city seize it and make it available to him. Where eminent domain laws

were once only used for the building of roads and hospitals, today this defined use has been broadened to include the economic benefit of just about anyone who intends to profit from your property. This law also means that developers who were once forced to offer people substantial market premiums for their homes are now more likely to offer them far less, because they know the homeowner will have little or no legal recourse once eminent domain is declared.

14) I saved the best one for last. In the past, wars have always boosted the American economy. World War II gave the U.S. economy such a shot in the arm that it led to the fabulous '50s, a time in our history when prosperity was at an all-time high. It actually solidified the strength of the American middle class. At this time, there's no clear economic evidence that the war in Iraq, or the war in Afghanistan has had any positive impact on the American economy. That is really an ominous sign. As any gangster will tell you, if you can't pump up the economy with a war, then something is very wrong.

CRIMINAL TSUNAMI

All of these ominous economic signs are converging to reveal a major downturn in the economy, and they are indicative of a fearsome trend—one that is fueling an unholy alliance born of the common goals and growing similarity in the business practices of organized crime and the corporate world.

What's happening is that many of the signs indicated above are being driven by an escalation in commercial ruthlessness, as well as a decreasing resistance to the aggressive and opportunistic behavior demonstrated by big business.

On the other side of the equation, we have what can only be described as a growing tsunami-like wave of criminal behavior that is coming at people from all sides. Wave after wave of corruption, fraud, malfeasance, and violence is now impacting Americans with such frequency that it is numbing their psyches and diminishing their desire to reject it.

This, in turn, has encouraged criminals and corporations to escalate their activities and learn from each other's tactics. The more successful they become at implementing modified versions of each other's business models, the more aggressively they push to redefine the envelope of what was once deemed inappropriate, unethical or illegal.

This "redefining" of inappropriate behavior is now something that is handled by professionals. In organized crime, it is accomplished with bribery and payoffs. Amongst corporations it's done with very aggressive governmental lobbying, designed to turn allegations of "fraud" into an acceptable "restatement of earnings".

All these circumstances are propelling our economy into a GangsterNomic future that is going to alter everything.

FORTRESS GANGSTORIA

There are now places on earth where the influence, sophistication and prevalence of organized crime has combined with the resources of big business to form such a powerful alliance that their governments must now assume a subordinate position to them.

Called "Fortress Gangstoria", this phenomenon results from the GangsterNomic merger and synergy which occurs when you combine the ruthless aggression of the criminal world with the ultra-sophisticated business models of the corporate sector.

You see Fortress Gangstoria regions in countries like Russia, Colombia, Asia, and the Middle East. What is

23

interesting is that they are now growing in some of America's major metropolises.

The pattern is almost always the same. In Phase One, the legitimate jobs disappear because of an economic decline or off-shoring. Next, there will be an increase in street crime, as well as an influx of drug dealers looking for new distribution points. The mountains of cash generated by the drug activity allows the people controlling it to acquire influence with the police and local politicians. This, in turn, allows them to escalate their criminal activity in ways that generate even more cash.

In Phase Two, the illegitimate activity has not only reached a saturation point, but is generating so much cash that a decision is made to begin acquiring legitimate businesses. As more of these businesses are acquired and placed under the wing of this criminal enterprise, they in turn begin to generate revenue, which enhances the economic strength of the criminals involved.

Now we enter Phase Three. At this stage, the criminal enterprise and its legitimate subsidiaries are now generating so much cash and influence, the politicians and judiciary on its payroll are both economically dependent on it and intimidated by it.

This leads us to Phase Four. Once we reach this phase, the stranglehold the criminals have over the politicians allows them to use their influence to dominate other corporations, which may pose legitimate competition to their own corporate subsidiaries. Once this happens, the amount of corrupt power and influence accumulated by them has become so immeasurable and impenetrable that it becomes fortress-like, hence the phrase Fortress Gangstoria.

While the Fortress Gangstorias one sees abroad have evolved into hybrid criminal / paramilitary / political entities, in the United States it tends to be a bit different. What's occurring here is that criminal organizations with mountains of drug money are investing those proceeds into legitimate companies. Their strategy is to eventually divest themselves of their riskiest criminal enterprises because of the increasing use of RICO (racketeer influenced corrupt organization) prosecutions to convict everyone in a criminal enterprise when one of its people is arrested.

The most interesting aspect of the entire Fortress Gangstoria phenomenon is the degree of impenetrability they are able to achieve. Let's take Colombia for example.

In the 1980s, the leader of the Colombian drug cartel was so powerful that he was the prime suspect in the killing of three Presidential candidates, the bombing of an airliner, and a military attack on a Federal courthouse designed to destroy all the court documents that resided within it. This is an example of a Fortress Gangstoria actually threatening the political power of an entire nation. It used its economic and paramilitary power to intimidate the government into assuming a state of ongoing fear and political impudence. Its impenetrability arose from the sheer quantity of people its organization had bribed and placed on its payroll.

In Russia today, the growing power base of some of its billionaire oligarchs is increasing at such a startling pace, the government is forced to seize their operations for allegedly failing to pay taxes. Some of these Russian and formerly Russian Fortress Gangstoria oligarchs possess such incredibly well-armed and trained paramilitary forces, they're able to mount long-term and occasionally successful battles against the Russian military. The impenetrability of these organizations arises from their access to heavy military equipment, as well as their possession of military-grade communications, intelligence and tactics.

In Asia, the Fortress Gangstoria phenomenon is quite common amongst the warlords that populate the various jungles of the Far East. The enormous revenues their drug operations generate allow them to finance extremely large and well-equipped private armies.

Most of these warlords have tasked their armies with two responsibilities. The first is to protect the manufacturing and distribution of their drugs. The second, and often more opportunistic, is to embark on operations that will allow them to expand their territories at the expense of competitors. Their impenetrability arises from their military power, geographic inaccessibility and fairly sophisticated intelligence networks.

Beyond their growing impenetrability, the Fortress Gangstorias located overseas have another characteristic which fuels their growth. As they accumulate corporations, the veil of legitimacy that their ownership creates causes a growing level of prosecutorial disinterest when it comes to investigating their illegal activities. It's almost as though no one in a developing nation is particularly enthusiastic about meddling with an entity that creates jobs and pays its bribes on time. This, in turn, just perpetuates their growth.

Criminal Business Model Fortress Gangstoria is a modern day criminal counterpart of the legitimate multinational corporate business structure seen throughout the marketplace. It possesses vast financial, security, marketing, distribution and political resources that it can deploy to the far corners of the globe in search of economic opportunities.

GangsterNomic Legitimate Business Model Alternative *The multinational corporate business structure is the legitimate counterpart of the Fortress Gangstoria business model. Its ability to defend its interests all across the globe with immeasurable resources all but assure its continued growth.*

MAY I POUR YOU A GLASS OF CRIMINAL ZEITGEIST

It's not just a coincidence that criminality has invaded so many areas of our culture, nor is it entirely a function of the profit motive.

A lot of the public's numbness and acceptance of the growing criminality they see around them is driven by the media's endless presentation of it for entertainment purposes. Here are some examples of the criminal zeitgeist that is encroaching on Americans:

Many artists are now releasing a title wave of CDs containing songs which routinely discuss killing police officers, raping women, selling drugs and making their money any way possible.

Video games containing violence now routinely generate more money than many motion pictures. Ironically, one can depict scenes in a video game like the tearing out of a human spinal cord during a brutal attack that most studios would be reluctant to include in an R-rated major motion picture.

Movie and television shows now contain so much violence that a growing problem is figuring out new ways to depict violence on screen in a manner that hasn't been seen hundreds of times before.

Some of the most popular new clothing lines are those which contain obscene phrases or pictures on them.

The highly militant self-shaved head look is so popular among young males now, it is affecting the earnings of barbers.

Automobiles are being fitted with stereos and bass speakers so loud that they can be heard approaching from several blocks away. This is clearly an effort to both intimidate others, as well as call attention to the power of the owner. This obnoxious form of acoustic intimidation is becoming so aggravating that many communities have passed ordinances banning it.

In and of themselves, none of these phenomenon are particularly meaningful. However, taken as a whole, they clearly represent growing evidence of the way that hostility and ruthlessness have somehow been mainstreamed into the soul of our society. This is the kind of desensitization that is paving the way for the future growth of GangsterNomics.

GUILTY BY REASON OF SANITY

As this new inverted morality spreads across the culture by rewarding ruthlessness and penalizing those who try to operate without it, it is clearly posing a conundrum for many people.

As they look about the economic landscape and see that those who demonstrate the greatest ruthlessness and commercial treachery are rewarded with the most success, it is only natural for them to ask themselves the following question:

Is it still possible to achieve considerable success in business without behaving ruthlessly? The GangsterNomic answer, of course, is that it is highly improbable.

The problem is, the playing field has changed. Our economy has devolved from one which operates under a set of laws designed to govern the propriety of commercial activity, to one which just appears to govern it, but really doesn't.

It is redefining the new meaning of economic insanity. That definition has now become: "Any profit made in the absence of a criminal conviction is now a legitimate profit."

SILENT ECONOMIC VIOLENCE

For several years now, the government and media have been discussing the potential damage to our economy that the next major terrorist threat will cause. Endless references are made to the economic damage done to the United States by the September 11th attack on the World Trade Center.

What very few analysts acknowledge is that a far more damaging form of silent economic violence is being directed at the U.S. It doesn't make use of explosions, power outages or plane crashes, yet its effect on the economy is far more damaging.

This silent economic violence is being directed on two levels. The first is a very systematic and methodical dismantling of our manufacturing and job base. The second is the ruthlessness and increasing similarity of the business models being employed by organized crime and our legitimate corporate sector. What makes it possible to characterize these as economic violence is the utter devastation they wreak upon their intended target.

Conventional terrorist attacks upon an American community may kill many people and destroy a great deal of property but time will pass and the community will heal, resurrect itself and come back stronger than before. That is part of what makes America great.

With this new form of silent economic violence it is much more difficult to recover once the attack has been carried out. If an economic enemy enters a one-industry town and shuts the plant down by sending the jobs overseas, then that city is devastated. The damage is often so severe, it then triggers an ongoing decline.

Just a few short years ago, analysts reviewed these situations and boldly proclaimed the dangers of building an entire community around one industry or plant. This suggests somehow that, if the city had only been wise enough to diversify, they could have easily survived the closing of their one major plant.

This silent economic violence has now grown and accelerated to such a level that it is devouring entire communities which are larger in scope and much more economically diversified. It is able to accomplish this not only by consuming factory jobs and manufacturing centers, but by displacing service jobs like accounting, radiology, customer support, transportation and many others.

There is even a movement afoot to allow individuals born overseas to come to the U.S. and become president. Think about that strategically for a moment. First, American jobs and assets are sent overseas, then a foreigner is brought over here to govern the entire nation. If that's not fulfilling the textbook requirements for invasion and conquest, then one would have to wonder what else it would require.

This GangsterNomic silent economic violence will only continue to escalate in the coming years. The information in this book is intended to help you survive and prosper during that coming cycle.

THE RISE OF SMART CRIME

As corporations survey the economic landscape, they are beginning to notice an unmistakable trend. What they're seeing is that the level of sophistication employed by criminal enterprises is not only growing, but in many instances it has surpassed that being demonstrated by the corporate world.

Most people are familiar with the sophistication of computer hackers and their ongoing effort to steal money. What they're not aware of, is an entire world of super-sophisticated criminal enterprises that are paving the way for their legitimate corporate brethren by developing new business models, technology, and much more.

Here are some examples:

Manufacturing – Motorcycle knockoff manufacturers in Asia are now using reverse engineering techniques so sophisticated that they are able to create copies of bikes that can't be distinguished from those made by the legitimate manufacturer without DNA testing. In September of 2000, Colombian police discovered a high tech submarine being built by a drug cartel in Bogota. Russian documents and technicians building the sub indicated that it was both state of the art and capable of transporting 200 tons of cocaine. These are just two examples of the recent quantum leaps in manufacturing sophistication that have been made by organized crime.

Distribution – Illegal copies of the latest Star Wars movie were reportedly available on the streets of New York the day it debuted in movie theaters. Some of the DVDs turned out to be of a quality that was better than anything investigators had previously witnessed. The logistics and technology required to make a high-quality bootleg DVD available on the same day it hits the movie theaters represents a significant advancement for the criminals involved.

Internet Fencing – Selling and distributing stolen and bootlegged items on the Internet has now been elevated to a science. The practice is so widespread, it has turned some legitimate online auction sites into the largest unwitting fencing operations in the world.

Counterfeiting – The growing sophistication of currency and document counterfeiters has caused a number of governments, including the United States, to make their currency more complex.

Market Manipulation – The ability of organized crime to seize control of entire markets in order to manipulate prices upward has been mirrored by the efforts of seemingly "legitimate" cartels to control their industry's pricing. What's interesting is how little legal scrutiny the "legitimate" cartels receive—a result of their political backing.

Election Manipulation – Many of the lessons learned from the successful election manipulation efforts of organized crime in the past have been modified, legalized and mainstreamed by some of today's political institutions.

DIARY OF A MAD BILLIONAIRE

Nations that most people reside in are not run by governments, democracies, Kings or Queens; they tend to be run by billionaires. It is the billionaires which create, finance and lord over the massive infrastructure covering the earth. Politicians may, from time to time, appear to be governing, but if they stray too far from the dictates of the men who financed their political campaigns, they too will find themselves out of work.

The majority of billionaires are good, decent, law-abiding men. They really don't need to break the law because, if a problem arises, they just pay for the introduction of a new law which makes the issue disappear.

The problem is that there are a few rogue billionaires who live for no other reason than to wage economic war on those of lesser means. Their entire lives are devoted to generating vast sums of wealth outside of the law, not because it is easier, but because it is more lucrative.

To cope with the economic assault of men like this, you have to understand how they think, because the only way to defeat a billionaire is to think like one. Here are some psychological tips and insights for understanding the thought processes which goes on in the minds of these men:

You're Not Human – Billionaires don't see you as human. At best, they see you as a client, a number or a demographic. At worst, you're seen as a minor inconvenience, standing between them and their next economic goal.

Your Lawyer Is An Insect In Their Hungry Eyes – Think you've really scored some points by having your lawyer file a lawsuit against a billionaire? Think again. Billionaires retain an army of lawyers and lobbyists whose full-time occupation it is to introduce, alter or eliminate laws which plaintiff's lawyers attempt to use against them. They will use this legislative influence to crush the independent lawyers who are suing them. It is not that you can't win in court when battling a billionaire, it is collecting your money that's almost impossible.

Money Is My God, My Religion And My Spouse – Make no mistake, money is the only thing these rogue billionaires understand, respect, fear and make true love to. Everything else is just cheap sex to them.

To deter the financially predatory efforts of these men, you must operate on the same psychological playing field as they do. That means joining forces with others to unite against this common economic enemy. If they are coming after your homes or businesses, then you must unite with a hundred others, and wage a political, economic and public relations war that will draw enough financial blood to cause them to reconsider their entire project.

Remember, if you lose the battle to hang on to your home, job or business, your life will then change dramatically. If the billionaire loses his battle to take one or more of those things from you, it won't affect his lifestyle at all. Tomorrow morning he'll still be drawing his next glass of water from the same five-thousand dollar gold faucet he drank from yesterday.

If you're clever enough, political enough, and determined, then you can prevail—you just need to start thinking in GangsterNomic terms.

DUMP THE THREE-PIECE SUIT—IT'S GANGSTERNOMICS TIME

It is not easy to change your business belief system overnight. Most people don't have the willpower to quit smoking, let alone initiate a major life change like this. But if you are determined, then let's begin. First, let's ask some fundamental questions about you:

Do you have a growing sense that it is becoming nearly impossible to conduct business honestly in the face of so much dishonest competition?

Have you been forced into bankruptcy even though you've tried to do everything right in your life?

Have you come to the conclusion that hard work, working smart and being your own man or woman will no longer get you to the economic finish line?

Have you come dangerously close to depleting all the equity in your home due to repeated refinancing?

Are you earning approximately the same or less than you did seven years ago?

Are you or your spouse working more than one job to earn less than you did five years ago?

Are more than a quarter of your friends unemployed or underemployed?

Did the events surrounding Enron, Tyco, Adelphia Communications, HealthSouth and Worldcom cause you to view corporate execs in a different light?

Has your company been driven to the brink of bankruptcy by overseas competitors offering low wages or slave wage labor?

If your answer to most of the above questions is yes, then you have met the first qualification for GangsterNomic enlightenment. You're aware that something is very wrong with the economy. More importantly, you sense that your hard work is not going to make it better.

EXTRACTING YOUR YUPPIE DNA

America has spent the last two centuries trying to convince its people that anything is possible if you just work hard enough. Decades of this rhetoric has created a generation of yuppies who feel that a college degree automatically entitles them to a $50,000 per year job and a $500,000 home a few blocks from the water.

The passage of NAFTA a few years ago combined, with the recent popularity of low wage labor in third world countries, has created a job market in the U.S. that can only be described as contractionary.

If you are to adapt to this new paradigm of diminishing economic opportunities, then you need to rid yourself of all those dated and irrelevant beliefs still echoing in your mind. It's time to shift into a GangsterNomic mode. Here are some perceptual changes you need to make:

Negative Home Ownership – You need to stop viewing homes as a place to live and start viewing them as a short-term investment opportunity that diminishes in value the longer you hold on to them. Forget about living behind the same white picket fence for the next twenty years. As the housing bubble bursts and values begin to decline, you need to keep a constant lookout for distress home sale opportunities. Don't just look at individual home sales, develop contacts with your local banks and credit unions as well. They're about to start repossessing homes on a massive scale. As many of these foreclosed properties become impossible to sell the banks will then come under tremendous pressure to liquidate the homes for little more than the balance owed on the mortgage. The real injured parties in this phenomenon will be the homeowners who hang on to their properties, thinking that if they just cling to them long enough, things will bounce back in a few years just like it always has in the past. Wrong move. To affect a recovery you need living-wage middle class jobs capable of supporting a family. Those jobs are now leaving the country so fast, the government is reluctant to institute any sort of hard accounting system to keep track of it all. They fear that reporting the actual numbers might unnerve so many people that it would only increase buyer apprehension.

View Vehicles Like Short-Term Stock Purchases – Chinese automotive manufacturers are now opening car dealerships in the United States designed to sell new vehicles in the six to eight thousand dollar range. Most automotive analysts believe it will only take a few years for Chinese vehicles to match the superior level of quality now seen in new Toyotas. This is noteworthy because most Americans tie their identity and self-esteem to the purchase price of their vehicle. Big mistake. If you are showing up for an important meeting, the kind of vehicle you arrive in does matter. Other than that you've got to start seeing cars for what they are—short-term investments with negative rates of return. If you absolutely must have something cool, then buy an old convertible sports car that is at least thirty years old. These cars will actually appreciate in value, and you can still enjoy driving them.

Start Viewing All Romantic Relationships As Business Relationships – Think this is going too far? Ask yourself how many yuppies lost their homes last year to spouses they've been married to for less than five years. You probably have friends you've known your entire life; maybe you even grew up with them in the same neighborhood. Do you think any of them deserve half or all of your home simply because you've known each other forever? Then what kind of antiquated logic makes you believe a spouse you've been sleeping with for a few short years deserves it?

Proactive Paranoia – Stop waiting for the shoe to drop, and just assume things are much worse than they appear. You will be so much better off that way. Have you ever seen a gangster who wasn't paranoid? Of course not. Each and every one of them walks around under the assumption that nothing is as it seems. The same can be said for many of the best CEOs.

The four psychological areas in which yuppies differ from gangsters most profoundly are in the way they view homes, cars, romance and money. Start viewing all four on a business level, and things will begin to change for you almost immediately.

Criminal Business Model Operating with a constant sense of paranoia, most gangsters employ various levels of security, surveillance and countersurveillance to minimize the outside threat. This usually involves bribing those that can provide useful intelligence.

GangsterNomic Legitimate Business Model Alternative Proactive paranoia means you will have to assume two things: the first is that constant and ongoing efforts are being made by your competition to compromise you economically. The second is that whenever possible, your competition will try to produce counterfeit knockoffs of your product or simply reverse engineer them. Criminal organizations are now employing digital manufacturing processes to make exact copies of complex counterfeit goods such as motorcycles, high-end fashion items and cameras. Often times it requires DNA testing to distinguish the difference between the products that come out of your factory and those made by counterfeiters.

TEN COMMANDMENTS OF GANGSTERNOMICS

Thou Shall Not Steal Anything Protected By Lawyers More Vicious Than Your Own – Coveting the assets of a fierce competitor is part of what has made capitalism great for so many years. What is changing is the ferocity and openness with which competitors are attempting to copy, appropriate, or just steal each other's products and services. It is not unrealistic to expect that after a highly profitable new product or service is brought to the marketplace, the average time for duplication or theft by an offshore competitor is probably less than thirty days. With newly released big-budget Hollywood movies, it is common now for bootleg copies to appear on the Internet the same day the movie premieres all across the globe.

Thou Shall Always Profit At Thy Competitor's Expense – Competitors exist for several reasons. The first is to provide you with ideas, products and services you can replicate and profit from. The second is to provide you with a great pool of employees you can attempt to hire away.

Honor Thy Diabolical CEO – The true measure of a CEO's value is his ability to extract market share from competitors who are even more ruthless than anyone thought.

Thou Shall Not Commit Managerial Blunders Without Publicly Claiming They Were Someone Else's Fault – This one is especially important when doing interviews with the national press. The greater the mistake, the more important it is to claim that it was initiated by some outside force completely beyond your control.

Honor Thy Corrupt Political And Legal Contacts – For it is they who will help you get out of hot water when no one else can.

Honor Thy Media Contacts – For it is they who will get you out of hot water that not even your political or legal contacts can help you with.

Thou Shalt Always Hoard Thy Cash – For it is only your cash that will get you out of problems that not even your political, legal or media contacts can help you with.

Honor Thy Competitor's Genius With A Job Offer Hiring great talent is one of the most cost effective ways to bolster your own revenues.

Thou Shall Move Quickly – Product-to-market cycles are now becoming shorter and shorter. There are some offshore product counterfeiters who can have knockoffs of your product out in the marketplace within forty-five days. If crooks with fewer resources than you and your legitimate company can do that, then why can't you launch your products more quickly?

Thou Shall Always Innovate – Whenever you are fortunate enough to encounter truly innovative talent, you should spare no expense to hire them. What do you think the salaries should have been for the folks who were hired to invent things like the cell phone, pager, rapid DNA test kits, etc.? Answer? Whatever it was, I'm sure a competitor would have paid them much more. One innovator can save your company and create an entire new industry. Don't insult these people with gold watches and $500 savings bonds. They deserve much more.

THE MONETIZATION OF RUTHLESSNESS

Ruthlessness has become a modern currency with growing economic value. If you have any doubt about this, all you need to do is consider how wealthy and accomplished most of the gangsters, corrupt CEOs and dictators around the globe have become.

Perform a comparative analysis of world leaders, corrupt CEOs, gangsters, hyperaggressive businesspeople, and athletes who consider themselves to be ruthless, and you will see a distinct correlation between their level of ruthlessness and the amount of assets they have accumulated.

What's interesting is that while ruthlessness was once considered a trait that placed one in a less than favorable light today it is revered. More importantly, possessing it can dramatically elevate one's market value.

If you perform a historical analysis of aggressive and imperialistic nations, they almost always acquire more assets and resources than their non-ruthless counterparts. Similarly, if you analyze the history of companies which have demonstrated hyperaggressive and ruthless monopolistic tendencies, you will also witness a massive accumulation of assets.

If one were to assign an economic value to the currency of ruthlessness by linking its monetary worth to the amount of assets its practitioner accumulates, then you would have a very accurate and quantifiable measure of its value.

Take a comparative look at some real-world examples below to get an intuitive sense for just how valuable the currency of ruthlessness is.

At one point during its ongoing narco battles with alleged drug cartel leader Pablo Escobar, the war between the cartel and the Colombian government was so ferocious that as many as 200 people a day were being killed in the capital city of Medellin. Not only was his alleged drug business continuing to thrive and grow, but a major U.S. business magazine declared him to be one of the wealthiest men in the world, with a net worth approaching three billion dollars.

After the turn of the century, industrialists began to build vertical monopolies designed to control every aspect of production in their industry. Their stranglehold on men, resources and pricing became so overwhelming, the United States government had to intervene with anti-trust and anti-monopolistic legislation designed to bring this unprecedented behavior to an end.

Given the many historical and modern day correlations between ruthlessness and success, it is probably fair to conclude that it plays a disproportionate role in the amount of financial success one may achieve.

WELCOME TO THE JUNGLE

Almost every one of history's most infamous gangsters was born into a situation which placed him at the bottom of the food chain. Drug cartel leader Pablo Escobar was born into so much poverty, he was reported to have begun his criminal career by stealing tombstones from cemeteries, sandblasting the names off, and then reselling them.

THE GANGSTERNOMIC BAPTISM

Before we go any further, we have to deprogram you. This GangsterNomics baptism ritual involves giving you a glimpse of ideas that are completely contrary to all the business concepts you have been taught. The old ideas may have worked back in the day when America still had jobs and opportunities for every person that got off the boat, but things have changed now. These unconventional ideas may cause you to shudder, but that's a good thing because it means you are re-aligning the foundation of your belief systems. Here we go....

GANGSTERNOMIC UNIVERSITY

If you are thinking about going to college and getting a degree in business, here's what you need to know. The vast majority of the classes, electives and degrees you will be offered by most universities will be a complete waste of your time and money. What most colleges and universities fail to tell you is that 80% of the people admitted as freshmen never receive a degree. Many of the people who do receive degrees never work in their chosen field. Most importantly, a lot of the folks who do graduate have accumulated so much tuition debt, their educational loan payments are now almost as expensive as their rent or mortgage.

Here are some other GangsterNomic facts to consider:

The wealthiest and most successful man in the world is Bill Gates. He started his company without completing his degree.

Most degree programs have a hiring rate so abysmally low, colleges refuse to post actual hiring rates on their web sites. They decline to do this because they know that if students saw how few jobs there were in some fields, no one would take those classes, and the programs and the revenue they generate for the college would collapse and disappear.

If you are thinking about getting a degree, then focus on one with a high probability of securing you a real job. Medicine, engineering, business, nursing and teaching are still degrees with very high hiring rates.

Law, computer science, radiology and accounting are degrees which are going to face horrific challenges in the coming years. Computer science majors will find themselves competing with foreigners offering the same skill sets for five cents on the dollar. Newly graduating attorneys are going to be facing tremendous competition from a legal marketplace that is rapidly approaching the saturation point with new attorneys, while at the same time being flooded with self-help legal software.

American hospitals are now hiring an increasing number of offshore radiologists who cost 85% less than Americans doing the same work. The hospitals will send their patient's x-ray images out over the Internet to their foreign radiologists who will review them and then email back their analysis. It's fast, cheap, and a growing cause for concern for a lot of American radiologists who thought they would go on earning $300,000 a year indefinitely.

Accountants and bookkeepers have faced tremendous challenges over the last few years because of the growing popularity of computerized accounting programs. The sophistication of these programs seems to be growing in leaps and bounds every twelve months. It is becoming increasingly difficult for sole proprietor accountants and bookkeepers to compete during tax season.

GANGSTERNOMIC INTERNSHIPS

If you are thinking about hiring, then one of the options you should consider is an intern. Senior level or even postgraduate students can be extremely competent and eager. What they lack in experience and knowledge they can often make up for by putting in extra hours.

Most companies make the mistake of hiring someone they think is the most competent person for the position. Don't make the mistake of always hiring the super-achievers, for they're often as conservative as they are anal. The proper

GangsterNomic approach is to hire someone who's both intelligent and possesses a degree of fearlessness. It's the boldness within them that will take them further than many other qualities.

One thing that many organizations do is characterize many real jobs as internships. This allows them to underpay the interns, while extracting the same amount of work from them as they would receive from a genuine staff member.

FORGET ABOUT RESUMES

Resumes are the new lottery tickets. They're a joke on those who can least afford it. No self-respecting gangster ever had a resume. There are more than a half a billion resumes available online worldwide. That means obtaining a job online is the statistical equivalent of gambling or playing the lottery. Do you think anyone actually reads them? The truth is that resumes are scanned by computer programs whose primary responsibility it is to eliminate unqualified applicants. The only truly innovative and realistic online technique for conducting job searches are performed by a company called **Insider Connections** (see **www.InsiderConnections.com**). They makes it possible for job seekers to develop and cultivate job contacts at companies they want to target with a job search. Everyone knows the best way to find a job at your target company is if you know someone there. InsiderConnections.com makes that possible by creating a free online marketplace which treats job contacts like currency and allows people to trade them at will.

Criminal Business Model Applying for jobs online has become a bit perilous in recent years because many criminal organizations have begun placing fake jobs ads online to lure applicants. They will then call them for an interview, give them a preliminary thumbs-up and tell them they need to fill out a "Background Check" form requesting their social security number, bank information, etc. Once

44

they have that, they'll empty the person's bank account and move on.

GangsterNomic Legitimate Business Model Alternative
As online job resume services are so inundated with millions of people, you are better off pursuing alternatives like InsiderConnections.com. It is a company which allows you to develop personal contacts at the company you would like to target with a job search. Since the best way to obtain a job is to actually know someone at the company you'd like to work at, InsiderConnections.com can make that possible.

NETWORKING GANGSTERNOMIC STYLE

Forget everything they tell you about resumes and networking in business school. No one is going to do business with you because they're impressed by the font style of your resume or because you play golf with them. That's the kind of nonsense that damages people's self-confidence when it fails to work. The reality is, it's just a ridiculous idea. Have you ever see a gangster do business with someone he met in a yoga class?

If you are going to conduct business networking you have to do it Gangsternomic style, and that means connecting with serious people.

Forget the stock investment clubs run by grandmothers hoping to make 8% on their money this year.

Forget about the neighbor who is trying to pitch you some ridiculous idea about opening up a coffee shop catering to singles.

Stay away from the freaks who've been watching the no-money-down real estate infomercials. Most of them will be working at the mall six months from now.

The best people in the world to network with are those who've made it once, lost it all, and are now trying to get back on top. These are the most motivated people on the planet. They had what it took to do it once. They lost it. Now they're fighting like hell to get back on top. You connect with ten people like this, and six of them will be millionaires again in five years.

Don't do what most unsophisticated people do, and ignore someone when they take a major financial hit. That can happen to anyone these days because there are so many variables in the business world. A real gangster knows that a guy who made it and lost it all is someone you have to take seriously, because not only do they have what it takes, but they have been humbled enough to be open-minded. This is someone you can approach.

Networking GangsterNomic style means connecting with people who have had it all, lost it and are now determined as hell to get back on top. They're serious, they're experienced, they're seasoned, and most important of all, they had what it took to do it once. Odds are they can do it again. One guy like this is worth ten thousand dreamers who've never accomplished anything but think they will.

WHERE TO NETWORK LIKE A GANGSTER

Forget all the other networking suggestions made by every business book author you've ever read. To network GangsterNomics style you have got to connect with serious people. Here's where you'll find them:

Bankruptcy Court Filings – Check out business bankruptcy filings that are at least a year old. By now the person has had some time to regroup and get a new plan in place. Reach out to this person through his attorney or through a private investigator. Tell him you respect what they've previously achieved and you would like to talk with them. Remember to qualify him first. Some of these guys aren't ready yet. If that's the case, then give him your number and tell him to call you when he's ready. The good news is, about half of them already had a new plan in place the minute the bankruptcy became final. Now it's a year later, and they have had plenty of time to implement it. These are guys you want to connect with.

Recently Fired CEOs, CFOs and COOs – A newly fired CEO is like a wounded lion. They're very dangerous because they're angry. Anger is an emotion that fuels a lot of powerful CEOs and gangsters. The difference is that most people are blinded by their anger, whereas CEOs and gangsters are fueled by it. Not only have they been to the top, but they know where all the corporate bodies are buried. Most corporations try to silence these guys with confidentiality agreements in their severance packages, but the truth of the matter is, you don't want their secrets. You want their abilities. That's what got them to the top, and that is what you need to capitalize upon. These guys tend to live in gated communities, so again you will need an attorney or private investigator to contact them.

Retired Professional Athletes – These are some of the most competitive people in the world. Now that they are no longer working as full-time athletes, most of them are constantly looking for business opportunities that make economic sense. A connection like this will not only give you credibility, but it will also open many other doors. They know what it means to put it all on the line, and they are fearless. Most of these guys are tougher than anyone you have ever met, so treat them with respect. You can reach out to these guys through their agents; many of them also set up their own web sites once they retire.

Former Hospital And HMO Senior Management – These folks let people who cannot afford their services die everyday. You don't get any more gangster than that. They're smart, ruthless, and most importantly, nothing gets in their way when it comes to making money. Hospitals and HMO senior management routinely kill more people in

47

a month than most criminal organizations do in a year, and nobody bats an eye. They exemplify the kind of new age country club ruthlessness that is shaping our economy. This is the kind of business connection that will keep you on your toes, because they look so disarmingly harmless. They look like the suburbanite who waters his lawn on the weekends while he's smoking a pipe, but make no mistake—this is usually a godless, heartless, MBA carnivore who would rather shut off your life support than let you get away without paying his hospital the $20 you owe him for the last aspirin you took. Gangster through and through—just the sort of person you can make money with.

Producers – These people are worth their weight in stolen credit cards. Movie producers, TV producers, radio producers; freelance or full-time, it doesn't matter. Whether they are local or national is also less important because they are all cut from the same cloth. They're super-sharp, ruthless, extremely well connected, and most important of all, they are the folks who know how to get something done. Walk onto a movie or TV set and you will see a group of creative people sitting around, endlessly debating some meaningless nonsense that has stalled the entire production. The producer walks in, and five minutes later the problem is solved. Things are back on track. Ask a billionaire who they want standing next to them when it hits the fan, and most of them will say they want a producer. CPAs are great for prepping your taxes, but if you want to create something of unique value and make certain it's brought to the marketplace quickly and professionally, or solve a problem in an entirely unique way, then you need a producer. Think of producers as highly creative freelance CEOs with the ability to create something of value out of nothing. That is a perfect description of intellectual property.

Pharmaceutical Reps – You have to love pharmaceutical companies. They are experts at hiring drop-dead gorgeous female sales reps who look like they just stepped off the set of a porno movie. They're all the same. Super ambitious, super hot and super anxious to sell their physician client any and every drug on the planet. What makes these connections so desirable is that these women can sell anything. I mean anything. If whatever you are working on requires impressive marketing or sales ability, these are the women for you. Doctors and dentists always joke about how bombarded they are by this onslaught of reps, but you would be shocked at how often the doctors buy their products. Even more hilarious is how effective these women are at getting the doctors to date or marry them. These are definitely the women you want on your front lines.

NIGHTCLUB VIP ROOMS—WHERE THE UNHOLIEST OF DEALS ARE MADE

Walk into any New York, Miami Beach or L.A. nightclub VIP room on a Friday or Saturday night and you are apt to see prominent people enjoying themselves. There are usually four things going on in the VIP rooms: drinking, drugs, women, and talk of deals the likes of which you will never hear on the golf course.

There's something unique about VIP rooms in a nightclub that seems to lubricate the deal-making process in a way that alcohol can't do anywhere else. It's not like VIP rooms are unique to nightclubs. They are also in airports, television and movie studios (in studios they're called green rooms), private clubs, etc. The ambience of nightclub VIP rooms seems to foster a unique atmosphere. It's almost a sense of "the people and celebrities here are special, so I had better tap into this while the moment lasts."

The alcohol, beautiful women, music, celebrities and overall atmosphere of coolness which seems to flow through the air creates a sort of temporary suspension of disbelief. That, combined with the hypnotic effect celebrities can have on businesspeople causes a heightened willingness to pursue opportunities.

You would be shocked to hear the sort of things that people will discuss in a VIP room. Once you get past the usual discussions about which waitress performs the best sexual favors, the topics almost always turn to money and business.

In Manhattan clubs, the discussions will range from Wall Street and finance, to industry-specific topics like real estate development or the media. The nice thing about the VIP rooms is that your mere presence in one usually announces one of several things: you're beautiful, wealthy, influential, or at the very least, a friend of someone who is.

If you're not a rock star or model, then chances are your seventy-thousand dollar a year civil service job affords you some control in the decision-making process determining who gets awarded multimillion dollar contracts by the city.

What is interesting about New York is that, while some of the people tend to be less recognizable than those in other major media cities, they are often extremely connected and all business. No matter how drunk or beautiful the women are, they are rarely likely to cloud the judgement of these dealmakers.

The other thing about VIP rooms is that the free flow of booze, drugs and women tends to create a sense of relaxed conversation that makes discussing something as intimate as money so much easier. It also has an odd effect on people's business ethics in that they will feel comfortable pitching or discussing ideas to each other that they would never do outside that room.

When celebrities begin to show up, things intensify. They'll begin doing things for shock effect just to impress some of the women in the room. On many levels, it just seems to increase people's propensity to talk business.

Because the volume of the music can be so deafening, gangsters and Wall Street creeps with more money than God will be openly discussing things they would never even whisper on the outside, for fear of being recorded. It's as though the bone-rattling music has somehow convinced them that they can't be heard.

In Miami Beach nightclubs the VIP rooms tend to be more hedonistic than New York. I think it has something to do with the hot weather. The women are also sexier. It's not just the tropical spice, but a modest sense of danger and excitement that seems to flow through the air, making things just a little more erotic.

Another thing about Miami Beach VIP rooms that seems to fuel the unsavory deal-making is the fact that the city seems to appeal to gangsters from every corner of the globe. Russian gangsters love it because the weather is so much more appealing to them than what they're accustomed to in Moscow. Asian gangsters love it because the women in Miami Beach are completely hypnotic. South American drug dealers come to Miami because it feels like a second home to them. They walk into some of the VIP rooms, and will start making contacts and doing deals with people just weeks after they arrive.

Los Angeles is the world capital of nightclub VIP rooms. Nowhere else on earth can you experience such an incredible number of places for money, power and beauty to connect.

Each year, thousands of people come to Los Angeles hoping to break into the entertainment industry. Some of them want to act, direct and produce. Most of them will take the conventional route and attend film school or an acting class while they work part-time waiting on tables. The really smart ones will make a part-time career out of cruising the VIP rooms. This is where the real fast networking track exists.

FIVE SECRETS FOR CRASHING VIP ROOMS

Nightclub VIP rooms exist for two reasons. The first is to charge ungodly amounts of money for exclusivity and prestige. The second (and equally important reason) is to keep out the unwashed masses which will try every trick in the book to gain access to the celebrities inside. Here are some tips and techniques for gaining access to the top VIP rooms:

Celebrity Accompaniment – One of the easiest ways to gain access to any VIP room is to walk in with a celebrity.

Paid Access – A number of high-end VIP rooms will grant you access if you simply pay the price. For many of these rooms, it can mean a minimal commitment of at least a thousand dollars in alcohol orders.

Back Stage Beauty Pass – Models are like currency when it comes to VIP room access. If you and your girlfriend are stunning, sometimes that's enough to get an invitation into this world.

Developing Relationships With The Club – Some club owners readily acknowledge the importance of all the business that is conducted in VIP rooms, and will encourage it. Developing a business relationship with these club owners or managers can yield tons of dividends.

Networking With Club Promoters – Club promoters tend to be very well plugged into the VIP party circuit. Their cell phones can be packed with the phone numbers of countless celebrities, businessmen and models just looking for a good time. On any given evening, a promoter can usually tell you what's happening where.

A few years ago there were a couple of sisters who moved to Los Angeles from Ohio. Without revealing their real names, we'll just call them "The Bombers". Both were aspiring actresses, and in addition to being extremely good-looking, they each had natural breasts that could only be described as circus-sized. If you saw them walking through Sunset's nightclub district, you would assume that someone was secretly filming a comedy and that these two girls must be wearing prosthetics, because no normal woman could possibly be built like that.

The Bombers could not go anywhere without being offered a career in porn. It was always ironic because they were incredibly straightlaced. They wouldn't drink, they didn't smoke, and they would never in a million years think of accepting money for sex, even though they were both earning modest money as waitresses.

Guys would get them auditions for straight acting jobs, but the casting directors could never take them seriously because their chests were so incredibly distracting.

They loved going out to the clubs and dancing whenever they could. VIP room bouncers loved them because celebrities would offer them hundreds of dollars if they could convince The Bombers to come in and join them. Eventually, the sisters became as appreciated and loved for their conservatism as they were for their physiques.

Then their lives took a unique twist. They met a couple of businessmen who offered them obscene money to work for them in a very unique capacity. They hired The Bombers to act as introducers. It turns out that Los Angeles is full of rich businessmen who are just dying to get a foothold in the entertainment industry, but were unable to do so.

In the past, pimps have tried to use prostitutes to open doors, but it never really worked because no one in their right mind would trust a hooker. The Bombers weren't prostitutes, though. In fact, one could make an argument that they might be the last two morally correct women in the city. That's what made everyone crazy about them, and more importantly, it's why people trusted them. These girls could get into any party, or have their call returned immediately by any executive.

L.A. was full of guys so rich and jaded that they barely trusted their mothers, but these same guys would turn into adoring fans whenever "The Bombers" walked in. I heard rumors that, at one point, the sisters were making as much as fifteen thousand dollars a week brokering meetings which made it possible for guys to get into entertainment circles they would never ordinarily have access to.

GANGSTERNOMIC CHAT ROOMS

If you are looking to conduct business online, then one of the options you may wish to consider are chat rooms. Before you proceed, let me caution you by saying that 99.99% of the people who frequent existing business chat rooms tend to be a complete waste of time. These rooms tend to be overrun by uneducated pranksters, multilevel marketing scamsters, and folks who are still bitter over the money they lost during the last dot-com bust.

If you are going to proceed, I recommend that you set up your own chat room. If you want to interact with serious and accomplished businesspeople or investors, here are some chat room names you may wish to consider using:

OFFSHORE BUSINESS NETWORKING

GANGSTERNOMIC CHAT ROOM

BUSINESS ROUND TABLE – NO SOLICITATIONS ALLOWED

(INSERT YOUR CITY NAME) INVESTMENT CLUB

INVESTMENTS I WISH I NEVER MADE – DISCUSSION
GROUP

These titles should provide you with a start. Needless to
say, the kind of chat room you start will be determined by
your business goals. As long as you keep your
expectations to an absolute minimum when dealing with
Internet chat groups you should be fine.

NETWORKING WITH BILLIONAIRES

The wealthy and powerful never go on vacation to network.
In fact, they will often avoid any attempts to discuss
business while they're vacationing. What happens is that
the super-wealthy tend to congregate socially in many of
the same locations around the world. When they do, they
strike up friendships they later remember when
contemplating future business opportunities and
partnerships. Here are some famous billionaire gathering
places. If you are going to do some very upscale
vacationing, you may as well do it in a place that is visited
by the wealthiest people on earth. At least this way there's
a possibility you can meet someone of substantial means
that you may do business with at a later time.

Mansion At The MGM Grand – Each of the thirty villas
has a pool, as well as original artwork by artists like
Picasso or Matisse.

Musha Cay, Bahamas – One hundred and fifty acres of
stunning exclusivity.

Le Toiny In St. Bart's, French West Indies – Twelve
stunning villas.

Turtle Island, Fiji – This exotic vacation resort was used
for the filming of both Blue Lagoon movies.

Frégate Island, Seychelles – Sixteen extraordinary villas occupied by movie stars and billionaires on a fairly regular basis.

The Wakaya Club, Fiji – It has eight bures (which can be described as thatched huts), and was reported to be the recent honeymoon location for one of the wealthiest men on earth.

Bedarra Island, Great Barrier Reef, Australia – Sixteen villas with open-air pavilions that have views of the ocean.

Huka Lodge, Taupo, New Zealand – Twenty extraordinary bungalows that have reportedly been stayed in by Queens and movie stars alike.

Little Palm Island, Florida – Twenty-eight stunning bungalows that are so appealing, former U.S. presidents have stayed there.

IT'S NOT WHO YOU KNOW, IT'S WHO YOU HAVE OVER A BARREL

A common misperception among businesspeople is the belief that, if you network with enough people, you will eventually connect with folks who can help you. Nothing could be further from the truth.

Simply networking with someone isn't going to mean they will actually help you. In fact, it almost never does. There are only two things which will increase the likelihood of someone helping you. The first is whether they believe you can also help them. The second is whether you've got them over a barrel because you've done them a favor in the past, or hoping you'll do them a favor in the future.

There are tons of people who constantly introduce themselves to others in the hope that it will eventually lead to business; it almost never does. To network effectively, you have to do it GangsterNomic style; for example:

Networking By Assistance – The minute you begin to network by asking for help, you are dead in the water. It is the last thing any businessperson wants to hear. What you need to do is begin by discussing what you can do for the person you are approaching. That is how you open up the gates of discussion.

Network By Contact-Building – Never approach someone and ask them to introduce you to someone else. You are in a much more favorable position if you approach someone and ask them if they would like you to introduce them to someone who may be of assistance to them.

Friendship Always Before Business – Never try to network with someone by making your business relationship more important than your personal relationship with them. Build the friendship first, and then, if the opportunity develops, pursue it with them on a business level. The greatest business connections and partnerships tend to be made by people who have been friends for a very long time.

Build Indebtedness – A very effective way to network is to build indebtedness by helping others. The more you help them, the more indebted and inclined they are to assist you in the future.

Criminal Business Model Criminals have two criteria when conducting business networking: 1) Can I make money with this person, and 2) How much of a threat to my personal safety will this potential partnership result in?

GangsterNomic Legitimate Business Model Alternative As a businessperson you should ask yourself the following: 1) Can I make money with this person? 2) What will the economic and litigation cost of exiting this partnership be? 3) Where am I most likely to connect with this level of individual? In many instances, these connections can be made in the VIP clubs of London, New York, Chicago, Miami Beach and Los Angeles.

EMPLOYING RETIRED JUDGES, POLITICIANS AND COMPETITORS

When networking or recruiting for highly ambitious projects, most employers tend to revisit the same sources they've always used to in the past: on-line employment services, headhunters, and internal candidates.

The proper GangsterNomic approach is to pursue potential candidates who reside outside the box; people others don't usually consider. If you have a major project that warrants such an investment, here are some out-of-the-box options:

Retired Judges – This is a great connection or job candidate for a wide range of reasons. Judges tend to have great political contacts, fantastic strategic vision, and the ability to grasp complex issues. Needless to say, they can provide invaluable insight into legal problems.

Retired Politicians – These people have outstanding connections as well as superior negotiating skills.

Retired Or Fired Competitors – This is a gold mine of opportunities. Few people can provide you with as much beneficial information and talent as one of your senior competitors.

An Imprisoned Competitor – The only thing more potentially beneficial than a retired competitor is one that is in jail. If they're behind bars, chances are their former employer has turned their back on them, and their options have severely diminished. Offering someone like this a consultancy while they are in prison will help them turn the bitterness and anger they feel toward their former employer into a stream of useful information that your company can benefit from. What better way to keep busy in prison than to help an ex-employer's greatest competitor destroy the company the inmate hates the most.

The Ex-Spouse Of A Competing CEO – This one you do for two reasons. The first is to milk them of any useful information they may have. The second is the sheer joy and great publicity one would create by having the newly divorced wife of your most hated corporate competitor on your payroll. What on this earth could be more satisfying than lording over the wife of a great enemy? The increase in his blood pressure, as well as the ongoing emotional torture this would inflict on him would be more than worth her salary. Now that's GangsterNomics.

PURCHASING GENIUS OVERSEAS

The current business fad of the day is hiring offshore employees such as laborers, engineers and accountants. What this practice overlooks is the real potential for profit. Hiring people like engineers, computer scientists and laborers will result in a wage savings that will incrementally boost your bottom line, but it will not have a transformational effect. It won't cause your company to make quantum leaps overnight. To do that you need genius.

Genius is still very expensive in the United States. Additionally, it has a propensity to go into business for itself the minute it has a great idea. The GangsterNomic approach would be to recruit from the top schools in India at whatever salary it takes to hire those students. Don't just make them an offer—tell them to interview everywhere they would like to work. When they're done interviewing, tell them to bring all their written job offers to you, and you will take their highest offer and beat it by 25%. This will be some of the best money you ever spent. The top schools are:

Top Five Indian Engineering Schools

Indian Institute of Technology, Kanpur
Indian Institute of Technology, Delhi
Indian Institute of Technology, Mumbai
Indian Institute of Technology, Chennai
Indian Institute of Technology, Guwahati

Top Five Indian Business Schools

Shri Ram College of Commerce, Delhi
Presidency College, Chennai
St. Xavier's College, Kolkata
Loyola College, Chennai
St. Xavier's College, Mumbai

Top Five Indian Schools Of Science

Presidency College, Chennai
St. Xavier's College, Kolkata
Loyola College, Chennai
Hindu College, Delhi
St. Stephen's College, Delhi

Simply gaining admission into the above universities means these students have outcompeted a hundred million others, and that's a considerable achievement in a country which values education as highly as India does. Hiring from these applicants will provide you with access to a gene pool of extraordinary geniuses. People who are more than capable of making the kind of breakthrough you need to leap past your competition overnight. It's the kind of investment you should consider making.

HIRING INEXPENSIVE OFFSHORE CRIMINAL TALENT

In a classic example of GangsterNomics, the world of organized crime has begun to copy the low wage business model being practiced by the corporate sector.

Just as corporations are scouring the earth looking for the lowest wage labor available, so too is organized crime searching for less expensive criminals. Not only is this a textbook convergence in business practices between the two worlds, but it is also indicative of the commonality with which they both view business.

Low wage offshore criminal talent is an enormous cost savings to organized crime groups involved in labor-intensive criminal operations such as boiler room telemarketing fraud, or manufacturing plants set up to produce counterfeit goods. In circumstances like these, a team may have as many as a hundred telemarketing fraudsters working the phones in different shifts to service multiple time zones, or a thousand factory workers producing fake tennis shoes or designer purses.

Another common use of low wage criminal labor are the farmers who grow the heroin poppy seeds of Afghanistan and the coca leaves of South America.

CRIMINAL CONCIERGE

Just as it is possible to retain a broker to help you put together a deal in the corporate sector, so too can you retain the services of a criminal concierge who will connect you with almost anything you need to commit a crime.

They operate under different names and work at different levels of the criminal world, but they each essentially do the same thing. For a fee they will connect you with people or resources that can help you commit a crime.

At the highest level of the criminal food chain are those concierges who act as intermediaries between the world of organized crime and the corporate sector.

SECRECY MERCHANTS

Secrecy merchants are individuals and groups who meet online to sell sensitive or stolen information. It may be a chat room dedicated to the sale of stolen credit cards and identities, or something far more complex.

This is an entire industry whose growth has been fueled by the Internet. Decades ago, you would have to know someone in the world of organized crime to deal with these people. All you need now is an Internet connection and the desire to visit a web site or an Internet Relay Chat room.

There are people out there selling information and access codes to just about anything you may want or need, and despite the repeated and aggressive attempts by law enforcement to shut them down, they continue to grow and thrive. Many web sites involved in this sort of activity are becoming accessible by invitation only.

The Secret Service recently announced that three of the most popular hacker / stolen information sites on the net had been shut down by them. The sites were alleged centers for major criminal activity. In shutting them down, law enforcement reportedly arrested nearly thirty people who were involved. Just one of these sites was reported to have trafficked more than a million stolen credit cards, which caused losses totaling many millions of dollars for the card owners.

Another recent news story reported that in the Ukraine there are regularly scheduled open-air markets and bazaars organized by people wishing to meet, discuss and trade stolen credit card information, as well as bootlegged movies, music and software. Apparently this has become such a huge growth industry that these bazaars have become very popular.

What's interesting about all this is that the degree of professionalism and technical sophistication possessed by these groups now rivals or exceeds that demonstrated by many of their counterparts in the world of legitimate business.

CONNECTING WITH YOUR INNER GANGSTER CHILD

As you prepare to make business decisions that you perceive to be ruthless, you will hear a voice in the back of your mind trying to talk you out of them. That's your inner anti-gangster child. It is the voice which is still trying to convince you that anything is possible if you just work hard enough and smart enough.

If that were true, then why are there so many Ph.D.s driving cabs in New York City? Why are there so many unemployed MBAs and CPAs? Why are there so many newly graduated attorneys working outside the legal profession?

The answer is that most of these people are listening to an inner voice that is no longer relevant. It's like bringing a knife to a gunfight. The world has changed, and they are just not properly equipped.

To properly connect with your inner gangster child you have to understand the concept of commercial ruthlessness. It is a very simple concept. Just ask yourself three simple questions: 1) Will this make money? 2) Is it legal? 3) Would I be envious if someone else came up with this moneymaking idea before I did? If the answer to all three questions is yes, then you should get started.

INTIMIDATION THROUGH PERCEPTION—THE POWER OF BLING

Criminals and CEOs routinely attempt to project power through the display of wealth. This is a tactic that was used as commonly by Alexander The Great as it is by most contemporary billionaires. Centuries ago, dictators projected power through the display of gold leaf and weaponry. Today such displays are referred to as "bling". The effect of their display is often as hypnotic as it is impressive.

Of course not everyone has the financial ability to "bling" on that level, but there are a number of GangsterNomic things you can do to impress prospective clients or business partners, even when your bank account doesn't.

First we'll start with some of the most obvious:

Vehicle – If you are going to an important meeting or presentation and your car just doesn't impress, borrow or rent one that does. There is nothing less impressive than showing up in a car that backfires when you step out of it.

Clothing – This one isn't as important as it use to be, but there are still some fundamental basics you have got to follow. Don't dress for the circumstance—dress for the audience. If you are meeting with millionaires who rarely wear socks, then don't wear socks. If you are meeting with lawyers in a Century City high-rise, a Hawaiian shirt probably isn't a good idea.

Jewelry – The solution here is do not wear any at all. There is one important exception though, and that is the watch—wear a really sharp watch. Understated, but still noticeable. The kind of watch that catches people's eye, and causes them to think you have great taste. Never wear a fake Rolex. A trained eye can detect one of these a mile away.

Celebrity Phone Calls – If you or someone you know has a celebrity friend, arrange to have them call your cell during the meeting. You can put the celebrity on your speakerphone and allow everyone in on the call just to impress them. Nothing impresses potential business partners more than being placed on hold because you have to take a more important call from a real celebrity. If you don't know any celebrities, there's a great company called **Hollywood Is Calling** (see **www.HollywoodIsCalling.com**), which will allow you to purchase a live phone call from a real celebrity for a modest fee. It will be the best money you will ever spend when it comes to closing a deal.

Beautiful Women – Nothing short-circuits the brains of prospective business partners or clients more than seeing a beautiful woman arriving with you. The key here is that while she's extremely stunning, she must also be dressed very conservatively. Any provocative clothing whatsoever will cause your new clients to assume the absolute worst about you. While officially she is there to assist you, in reality she's there because the company of a beautiful woman projects a subtle display of both power and success, and that is how you want to be perceived.

Free Meal Or Drinks – If you are meeting clients or a prospective business partner at a restaurant, arrange to get there early and give the manager your credit card for a pre-authorization. Then arrange to have him come by your table during the meal and express his extreme joy and gratitude at the fact that you have taken time out of your busy schedule to patronize his restaurant. Then have him tell you what an honor it is to have you there, and that the meal is on the house. Later you can slip away to the bathroom and go sign the credit card slip for him. Make sure to include a very nice tip.

EXPLOITING UNFAIR ADVANTAGES

The amount of value you can extract from a commercial activity is directly linked to how advantageous your position is during the negotiation or transaction. The greatest value can be obtained from total advantage. While some would characterize total advantage as an unfair advantage, the reality is that if it is legal, it's fair. It just seems unfair when the other side is holding all the cards.

There are a number of techniques one can use to obtain an unfair advantage. Here are a few:

Inside Information – Obtaining information that few others have and using it to pursue an economic opportunity is perfectly legal under most circumstances. It is not legal when it involves stock trading, but it's perfectly legal when it comes to scenarios like offering to purchase property before it is listed because you know the owner is planning to sell in the near future. In fact, there are many people who have built fortunes on the acquisition of real estate before it was listed. Inside information can be obtained from a myriad of sources, including friends and business associates.

Economic Strength – Great advantages flow from the economic disparity between buyers and sellers. Major retail buyers will often use their economic clout to extract enormous pricing concessions from vendors. The only way to combat such pricing demands is to take your product elsewhere, or distribute and sell it yourself.

Technical Advantage – Developing a technical innovation that destabilizes a market will create a tremendous advantage. When peer-to-peer file swapping technology was invented to allow people to instantly and freely exchange songs online, it almost brought the music industry to its knees. At the 2006 Consumer Electronics Show, Google announced it would be launching its Google Video Store, a service that would allow anyone to post their video content online and sell it at any price they like. The content producers have the option to offer their content on a download-to-own or download-to-rent basis. Some experts believe that Google's enormous new video distribution system will eventually pose a serious threat to existing movie and video distributors.

Unfair advantage is just an economic synonym for "you have more clout than I can oppose." No one possessing an unfair economic advantage ever claimed it was excessive. Those allegations are always made by the weaker party attempting to strengthen their position.

Pricing is not the only way to exploit an unfair advantage. You can leverage your unfair advantage to secure better distribution, marketing, delivery dates, return policies, payment terms, shipping costs, insurance costs, litigation settlement terms, etc. With enough unfair advantage, there is almost no end to the terms and conditions one can insist on (and often receive).

ABUSING YOUR POWER INTELLIGENTLY

Exploiting an unfair advantage only makes sense if it doesn't destroy the opportunity you hope to capitalize upon. Many organizations that have secured an unfair advantage fail to notice that an invisible threshold exists. It is a line that you should never cross by making a demand so unreasonable that it destroys the business relationship you have. Sometimes it is crossed by making an absurd pricing demand; other times it can be overstepped by taking so long to pay a vendor that it damages them financially. There are some industries which are notorious for taking as long as twelve months to pay vendors or original equipment manufacturers. They'll delay payment as long as possible to earn extra interest on their money. Unfortunately, this creates so much ill will and financial hardship that many of their key business relationships are just a breath away from collapsing.

Abusing your power intelligently means deriving as much benefit as your circumstance will allow you to exploit, without passing the economic point of no return. Never make economic demands that prevent a vendor or business associate from walking away with some profit.

A classic example of this is the gas station industry. While most gas stations are owned and operated by independent businessmen, the per gallon price at which their gasoline is bought and sold is often dictated by oil companies.

A few of these companies have left so little profit margin in the resale of gasoline to the station owner, it is causing two things to occur. The first is that most gas station owners have now incorporated convenience stores/grocery stores/restaurants into their businesses to generate other revenue streams. The second phenomenon is a bit more insidious.

Because they are making little or no money on their gasoline sales, a growing number of gas station owners are shorting their gas pumps. This means that every time you purchase a gallon of gas, you are actually receiving 20% to 50% less. Instead of receiving a penny or two in profit for each gallon of gas, the station owner is raking in hundreds of thousands of dollars each month in illicit profits.

If you think that's an exaggeration, take an empty one-gallon container and visit three or four of your favorite gas stations. Pre-purchase exactly one gallon of gas at each one, and then try to fill your container to the one gallon mark. If it is off by ten percent, that's an extra quarter in tax-free profit the owner makes on each gallon. If it's shorted by as much as half a gallon, that is easily another $1.25 in the pocket of the station owner.

If you think it's just a coincidence that you've been shorted at several stations, try visiting another fifty gas stations to see if any of those "miscalibrated" pumps puts more than a gallon of gas in your container. It is highly unlikely. Fraudulent behavior like this is caused by the unintelligent abuse of power.

Another factor to keep in mind when attempting to abuse your power intelligently is that the abuse must always be legal, and should occur purely for financial gain. It must never be done for emotional or punitive reasons. The problem is, this line often gets crossed by people abusing their power, simply because doing so inflates their egos. It's usually the beginning of the end for the abuser.

If you are going to abuse your power intelligently, make certain there are sound business reasons for doing so, and be careful not to permanently damage your trading partner.

ELEVATING YOUR MEDIA PROFILE

One area in which the world of organized crime and the corporate world differ significantly is in their use of the media and publicity. With a few rare exceptions, most gangsters avoid the limelight because it generates too much interest in activities they would like to keep secret. Corporations, on the other hand, create and pursue media attention very aggressively.

Part of what establishes your value in the marketplace is how well you are known and perceived. If you're interested in increasing that value, one way to accomplish it is with media exposure or self-promotion.

Many municipalities have local access cable channels which allocate a certain percentage of the airtime to programming produced by or for citizens. This is a great way to get some studio time to produce content or promotional material that you can use to call attention to yourself or your projects.

Many of these studios are staffed by people who will surprise you with their great work ethic, talent and ambitiousness. Approach this opportunity intelligently and you can turn it into a major asset.

Another thing you can do to call attention to yourself or your project is to pay a celebrity to pose in a photograph or video with you. This will automatically render the image or video more noteworthy, and increase the likelihood of the media taking an interest in it.

THE ZOMBIEFICATION OF THE AMERICAN WORKER

America has the brightest and hardest working workforce in the world, but look around at what is happening and you will see our unemployed workers being treated like zombies with resumes.

Companies don't want to hire unemployed workers. Government statisticians do not acknowledge their existence after their unemployment checks run out. New employers now run credit checks on job applicants as part of their background check. Think about the insanity of that for a moment. If a person is out of work, then logic would dictate that they probably have credit problems. Why even bother checking? Some of the companies that do this will tell you there is a corollary relationship between how financially responsible a job applicant is, and how well they perform their job responsibilities. There might have been a grain of truth to that back in the 1950s, but our current economy and job market is so fractured and unpredictable, the only thing bad credit indicates is that you have bad credit. It does not indicate why your payments are late, hence there is no way to make any useful inferences from such information. If this isn't bad enough, watch what happens when an unemployed individual tells their new date they're unemployed.

These are the kinds of growing economic realities the American worker is now facing. They are also the kinds of forces that have given rise to the new hyper-Darwinian GangsterNomic paradigm.

PROFITING FROM THE COLLAPSE
OF THE JOB MARKET

There is only one thing you need to know about your first, next, and last job, and that is it should serve only one purpose. That purpose is to teach you as much about your employer and his business as possible so that you can start your own company. If you are going to be a proper practitioner of GangsterNomics, you have to understand that, statistically speaking, you will never really get ahead working for a corporation.

Given the accelerated rate at which the American job market is collapsing, it is important to become financially autonomous as quickly as possible, and that means self-employment. Absorb as much as you can from your first few employers, then make it a point to launch your own business as soon as your circumstances allow. Establishing your own financial autonomy will help insulate you from the collapse of the job market, and allow you to reap the greatest rewards.

CLIMBING THE CORPORATE LADDER
GANGSTERNOMIC STYLE

When you start a new job you will hear all the usual non-sense about excelling at work. They will have some forty-five-thousand-dollar-a-year human resources rep give you pamphlets and sit you down for an orientation. If you're really lucky you will have some pot-bellied middle manager (who has had the life sucked out of him by his last three divorces) latch on to you as your unofficial company mentor. He will break up the monotony of his workday by proudly walking you through the intricacies of avoiding this week's latest round of layoffs.

You will hear about the importance of working long hours, being a team player, and getting along with people. You'll receive countless emails, memos and presentations on the importance of being competitive, lowering costs, tracking the competition, and reverse engineering their hottest new product which they no doubt just stole from someone else.

If you're involved in sales you will be confronted with an endless parade of chain-smoking, liquor drinking, pill popping sales managers in endless pursuit of this month's sales quota, so that they can hang on to their stripper girlfriend for one more week. Their mind-numbing mantra will always be "We Need To Get These Sales Figures Up".

If you are in accounting then your CFO will no doubt pressure you to cut costs even more this month. Presumably, the 10,000 offshore workers the company hired last month for fifty cents an hour haven't lowered operating costs sufficiently.

Wherever you go in corporate America, the mantra will be the same—we need to figure out how to get more for less.

A proper practitioner of GangsterNomics understands that this is all just blue smoke. He understands that, in order to launch himself up the corporate ladder, he has to do it gangster-style. It means bringing himself to the attention of senior management.

How do you do that? You do it by offering them something unique or potentially very profitable. Bring them an idea or an opportunity they had not considered. What you do will depend on your industry and situation, but I can assure you that one well written proposal or innovative idea will get you far more attention than ten years of showing up for work on time and coming into the office on weekends like every other plow horse with alimony payments.

The ideas don't even have to be brilliant. They just need to get you noticed, and help distinguish you from the other wage slaves in your office.

Eventually, one of your superiors will call you into his office to discuss how much he loves your ideas, and how he wants to congratulate you for saving the company so much money.

This is the crucial moment. This is the moment when you look each other in the eye, and both of you know the dynamic is shifting. Your supervisor realizes that senior management now has you on their radar, so he will have to treat you with a few more ounces of respect. But he also needs to take credit for your accomplishments so that he can capitalize on your hard work.

This is the pivotal moment in which you strike.

First, you thank your boss for the compliment. Then you look directly into his eyes, and say how thankful you are to be acknowledged by someone with his experience, and that you look forward to contributing to this great company in any small way you can.

OFFICE POLITICS WITH A GUN

Few things ignite (or end a career) faster than office politics. Surviving and thriving in a corporation is not unlike achieving the same in a criminal organization; the only difference is that the stakes are much higher. Make a mistake in the office and you are likely to see a couple of negative comments on your next quarterly review. Screw up in a criminal organization and you're apt to get invited to a knife fight.

How you ascend the hierarchy in both the criminal and corporate world is often determined by the temperament and style of the leadership. Dictators like Joseph Stalin allegedly killed subordinates who demonstrated even a hint of ambition or independence. That sort of behavior is usually born of tremendous insecurity.

In the corporate world, a few past auto company leaders were rumored to have been notorious for promoting subordinates who, when they did eventually ascend to power, performed so unimpressively that they made the current leader look spectacular.

Conversely, a number of major Wall Street investment banks are legendary for hiring people they feel represent the absolute best the industry has to offer. Something you'd think would be fairly common amongst other CEOs, but is actually quite rare given how often their egos affect their strategic decisions.

TIPS FOR SURVIVING BRUTAL OFFICE POLITICS

Become your bosses eyes and ears. Cause him to become dependant on the information you funnel back to him about some of the other activities in the company. Try to create the ongoing impression that there's a lot going on outside his office door and that you'll let him know about it as soon as you do.

Treat your boss's boss as an even greater opportunity for job preservation. You can also engender his respect and appreciation very effectively by helping him obtain positive press or the acknowledgement of his superiors.

Criminal Business Model *Surviving politics in a criminal organization is often a function of as much animal cunning as it is brute force.*

GangsterNomic Legitimate Business Model Alternative *Surviving politics in a corporate setting is often a function of aligning yourself with, and mirroring the temperament and tendencies of your superior.*

WORK FOR AN ENTREPRENEUR INSTEAD OF A CORPORATION

Another option is to work for an entrepreneur. If you are at an early stage in your GangsterNomic career and thinking about working for someone else, here is what you need to know: corporations are set up to hire workers, not businessmen. In fact, many of them won't even hire you if they find out you were previously an entrepreneur. They will tell you it is because they are concerned about your ability to take orders; but in reality, it's because they know you're too similar to them.

Their corporation was probably started years ago by someone who thought he could improve upon what his employer was doing, so he went into business for himself and began competing against them. Now they're afraid you will do to them what they did to someone else decades ago.

That is why it takes five vice presidents, twelve division heads and three committees to order a paperclip in a corporation. Everyone is petrified of acting too independently because they know how threatening that is to the leaders who run the place. So what do they do? They all huddle together to obtain a consensus. That is why corporations love meetings and entrepreneurs hate them.

Entrepreneurs love to get things done, and they instinctively understand that meetings are hiding places for group thinkers who are very risk averse. Show me a consensus builder and I'll show you a group thinker who never had an original idea in his life. This is the kind of guy who thinks he's going out on a limb just by reading a book like this. Stay away from them. These people are a khaki-pants-wearing, latte-coffee-drinking cancerous growth on the great gangster spirit of America. They are responsible for the mess America is in now. You see them everywhere you go. They're the creeps that try to bond with you at a party by striking up a golf conversation just before they try to sell you something. This is what happens to guys who lose too many fights on the playground—they turn into metrosexual salesmen.

GETTING FIRED GANGSTERNOMIC STYLE

America's new favorite corporate sport has become firing people. They get fired for every imaginable reason under the sun, and often times for no reason at all. Firing people has also become the new ballistic career path of choice for aspiring middle managers wishing to someday become senior management.

The one thing most people in the workplace have in common is that they will all someday be fired. It may be called a layoff, downsizing or a transition, but the end result will be the same. They will be out there looking for work again.

Before this happens to you, there are some things you can do to strengthen your position. If you think you are going to get fired for an inappropriate or unlawful reason, you should consider doing the following (consult with your attorney prior to doing anything, to make certain you are not violating any laws).

Discretion – Before you even consider taking any action, you need to understand how important it is to be discrete. If you are going to meet with an attorney, do not disclose or discuss it with coworkers. Tipping your hand by letting your superiors know your strategy may get you fired prematurely, so be very careful.

Wear A Digital Recording Device – You can purchase a digital recording device now that is no larger than a pack of cigarettes. They're fairly inexpensive, and some of them can record up to eight hours. They're digital, so you can download the audio files onto your hard drive via a firewire or USB cable. If you are able to record your superiors saying or doing something inappropriate, this may strengthen your case should you decide to sue for unlawful discharge.

Form A Coalition – Seek out others who have been, or will be fired soon, to determine if you can share any information that may be of benefit to you as a group.

Document Everything – Keep a very detailed log of everything that transpires. Include dates, times, places, names of other people present, etc. This will also strengthen your case should you decide to take legal action.

Meet With The Media – If your employer is involved in unethical or illegal behavior that is impacting the public or involves tax dollars, the media may express an interest in your story. Involving them may increase your leverage.

Investigate Any Racial Or Reverse Racism Component – It is illegal to fire someone in the United States for racist or reverse racism reasons. If you feel this is the case in your circumstance, you should seek legal counsel.

Getting fired is one of those life experiences that tend to be unfortunate for everyone involved. However, no one should be fired unjustly. Far too many people simply take it on the chin and go on with their lives. If you feel you've been fired unlawfully then you should meet with an attorney.

If you think your situation at work is perilous, then under some circumstances it is possible to negotiate a severance package that will ease your exit. If that's the case, the company will often require you to sign a release which bars you from taking any legal action against them in the future.

BUSINESS PARTNERS ARE LIKE FUTURE EX-WIVES

Thinking about going into business with someone? Do it GangsterNomic style. The first GangsterNomic rule of selecting a business partner is one which every gangster throughout history has understood. Ask yourself what happens when this thing goes bad, because sooner or later it will. Meyer Lansky did it when he partnered up with Bugsy Siegel. Most rich guys do it with the women they date. Partners are great. They're fantastic. They bring qualities to the table that help you accomplish your goals. The problem is that statistically speaking, your partnership is eventually going to end. Before that happens, you have to be able to ask some tough questions:

1) Can I beat my partner in court? Right or wrong has nothing to do with it. The only question that matters is who has the resources to win a prolonged and expensive court battle. If you don't think you do, then this is something you may wish to consider.

2) Is your prospective partner someone you can control?

3) If I do partner up with this individual, will I gain enough from the situation to offset the future cost of severing this partnership? The bottom line is not what you make during the partnership, but what you hang onto after it is dissolved.

If you have performed this cost-benefit analysis and determined this is someone you want to partner with, then you are ready to proceed to the next level.

SIX GANGSTERNOMIC RULES OF PARTNERSHIP

Set Up Dual Account Streams On Day One – This is much easier than it sounds, but is rarely done because most businessmen are like newlyweds—deep down inside they want to believe their partner won't screw them over, so they set up a single accounting system. This is as big a mistake in marriage as it is in business. When the revenue begins to flow you need to pay your operational expenses and accounts payable, and then split the net dollars right down the middle and deposit them into separate accounts. The accounts should be completely separate and signature-accessible by only one partner. Any new or existing partner who objects to this can not possibly have any legitimate reasons for doing so.

Ghost Marriage Partners – If you start a partnership with a business partner who is single and then decides to get married, then you will (whether you like it or not) be forced to endure the involvement of a ghost partner. This new spousal ghost partner was not involved in any of your original business efforts, but will now possess a growing influence over what you and your business partner do from this point forward.

Hire A Private Investigator – If you are going to go into business with someone, hire a private investigator to check out their credit report, cash flow, litigation history, debt structure and, most importantly, do the same for their spouse. I've seen instances where partners will go into business, poach the assets of a fast growing company, and then try to hide the stolen capital goods or funds from their partner by placing the assets in the control of a relative.

Be Careful In Florida, Nevada And The Caribbean – These places seem to attract tons of con men, boiler room operators, drug dealers, money launderers, investment advisors with multiple felony convictions, financially predatorial women who get married every time someone offers to buy them a cheeseburger, real estate shysters, mobsters from Russia, Eastern Europe, Central America and Asia, pyramid schemers, prostitutes who work as part-time real estate agents, etc. Don't get me wrong, these are great places to visit; however, it is difficult to spend more than a few hours in any of those locations without all sorts of people coming out of the woodwork wanting to show you a new investment opportunity. I once heard a story from a guy who was sitting with his girlfriend at a very upscale outdoor café on Ocean Drive in South Beach, Miami. Ten minutes after they sat down, they noticed that a guy at the next table was being approached every few minutes by people who appeared to be very discretely buying drugs from him. This went on for about a half an hour. Then a couple came by and joined the dealer at his table. They made small talk for a couple of minutes, and then the drug dealer whipped out a prospectus for a new real estate partnership he was putting together. The couple signed some papers, pulled out their checkbook and wrote him a check. This is what I'm talking about—these are the people you have to avoid. GangsterNomics isn't about doing business with criminals. It's about understanding the most aggressive, ruthless and successful business principals employed by corporate criminals, dictators and thugs, and then adopting a modified version for one's own legitimate business endeavors. The beauty of this book is that it equips you with the tools to make it possible.

Know The Astrological Sign Of Your Business Partner – There are certain astrological signs that are predisposed to disreputable behavior. That's great if you're a gangster, but it's really bad if you are looking for a partner. There are dozens of astrology books that can help guide you on this level. Before you laugh too loudly, let me tell you a story. A few years ago, a major business publication interviewed a number of Asian billionaires and asked them if they employed astrology to make their business decisions. Most of them said yes, but added that while they did not allow astrology to be the final determinant of their decision, they would never be foolish enough to dismiss it. It is common knowledge that astrology has been used by U.S. presidents. Knowing your prospective business partner's astrological sign and having their chart done will tell you more about them than running their credit report.

Consider All Partnerships Temporary – From the first day you begin working with your new business partner you should be proceeding along two tracks. First, focus on building the business as aggressively as possible. Second, lay the groundwork for how you will proceed after the dissolution of the partnership. Most partnerships are ended by greed, mismanagement, theft, incompetence, strippers, hookers, drugs, fraud, quarrelsome spouses, too many trips to Vegas, etc. Whatever the reason, you should be prepared.

Criminal Business Model Criminals rarely trust partners they have not committed a major crime with in the past, or known since childhood. Many will actually require a prospective partner to commit a violent crime upon an unsuspecting third party just to make certain they are not involved with law enforcement. This is what some major police departments now suspect is the reason behind the dramatic increase in the random and unprovoked shootings of so many innocent people.

GangsterNomic Legitimate Business Model Alternative – In addition to all the conventional background and reference checks, you should also isolate or compartmentalize your partner's access to your business accounts until you are completely comfortable with them. It can also be very helpful to have your prospective partner's astrological chart done to let you know if there will be any problems.

BUYING A BUSINESS PARTNER

This is a classic GangsterNomic move. Some prospective business partners can not be enticed into going into business with you by the sheer promise of potential wealth down the line. If having them on your team is so important that you cannot let them go, then you may have to purchase their involvement.

MICRO-PARTNERSHIPS

Most people view partnerships as long-term commitments. In the world of GangsterNomics, forming a business relationship that exists only as long as the project does is called a micro-partnership.

Micro-partnerships have a number of benefits. First, they are compartmentalized. This means that your work, liability, time and involvement together is limited to just one project. When that is concluded, the partnership is concluded. Secondly, micro-partnerships tend to be less complicated because their economic focus is much narrower in scope.

NUKING A BUSINESS PARTNERSHIP

What do you do if you are involved in a business partnership that you want to dissolve? Assuming it cannot be dissolved amicably, you have a couple of GangsterNomic options:

A Shotgun Clause – Every partnership agreement should include a shotgun clause. This is a buyout clause that allows one partner to buy out the other for "X" number of dollars. Without a shotgun clause, arriving at the buyout valuation is always tricky because the buyer always wants to lowball his partner with an offer that is well below what he really knows the partner's equity to be worth. The beauty of a shotgun clause is that it forces honesty upon both partners; it gives the partner you offer to buyout for "X" number of dollars the right to buy you out for the same amount. This prevents partner A from offering a hundred thousand when he knows it's worth ten times that. If he realizes that doing so could trigger a shotgun clause that would allow partner B to buy out partner A for the same amount, then he will be forced to make an honest offer to prevent his own equity from being snatched away for pennies on the dollar. It's beautiful and it keeps people honest.

Pre-emptive Dissolution Clauses – These clauses can be included in your original partnership agreement and will detail the exact terms of any dissolution.

The Nuclear Option – This is an option most commonly used by gangsters, dictators, celebrities, major corporations, and just about anyone with more money than scruples. The nuclear option is where you completely disregard right or wrong as well as the terms of the partnership agreement and simply declare litigation war. You have your lawyers blast away for as long as it takes. Drive your ex-business partner to an economic point of diminishing returns—the point where his cost of continued litigation begins to dwarf whatever he would have gained economically by continuing to battle you in court. This is as gangster as gangster gets. It's about as close to legal extortion as you will ever see, and probably why it's so popular. You have to be careful with this one though. Lawyers love it because it works one out of three times, but every once in a while people who have had it happen to them go off the deep end. They literally grab a meat cleaver or shotgun and go after their former partner and his lawyer. They will leap out from behind some bush when you least expect it, and come after you with a rusty knife they've been dipping in excrement all day. People in gated communities love this option because they're seldom at personal risk (but even they have been gotten to). You would be shocked at how dangerous a suicidally depressed ex-business partner can be if he has just lost everything in court. Given how often this option is used, the real miracle is that more people don't get killed by it.

SELF EMPLOYMENT—GANGSTERNOMIC STYLE

Most of history's major criminal organizations, corrupt corporations and political dictatorships were started by someone who hated working for someone else. It's as simple as that. If you are about to consider self-employment, let me tell you what you need to know.

When Lucky Luciano formed Murder Incorporated, it became an organization many believe was responsible for the murders of thousands of people from coast to coast. Conventional wisdom was that the murders were necessary for the preservation of their organization, as well as the pursuit of its economic goals. In reality, its motive was far more fundamental, because all criminal organizations and cartels exist for one reason and one reason only—they exist to control rather than be controlled.

If you are going to consider self-employment, you should adopt some of the criteria that criminal organizations use when they decide to go into a business:

Look For Weakness – The GangsterNomic view of all economic weakness is that it presents an opportunity. The greater the weakness, the greater the opportunity. Survey the economic landscape and look for problems. Be open-minded, and most importantly, be willing to go in a direction others are fleeing from. Believe it or not, there are a number of fast growing cleaning companies in the United States that specialize in cleaning up crime scenes. Murder scenes, suicides, industrial accident sites, you name it— they clean it. Nothing deters them. They will go into a bedroom and clean brain matter off the walls five hours after some poor guy stuck a shotgun in his mouth. They'll do this because they can charge a ton of money to perform a service that would cause most people to seek out a psychiatrist. This is a classic GangsterNomic example of converting adversity into opportunity.

Select Opportunities The Big Money Hasn't Exploited Yet – It usually takes a few years for large slow moving companies and investors to recognize a new opportunity before the big dogs move in and eat the little dogs. Remember all those mom-and-pop video rental stores that disappeared overnight when the massive video rental chains opened up next to them? Same principal.

Failures Are Profitable – Just as people can make money in the market when a stock starts to dive, so too can GangsterNomics allow you to profit from failure. Look for opportunities that will allow you to service the failures of others. Believe me, this will be a huge growth sector. There are investment advisors out there who pray for new factory closings. They will obtain a list of all the newly laid off workers and then approach them with countless investment opportunities. There are bankruptcy lawyers who foam at the mouth every time interest rates go up because they know it means more defaults, which usually results in more bankruptcies. There are companies in the Midwest which specialize in auctioning off the heavy equipment being sold by newly bankrupt tool and die shops. Most of their clients are the Chinese companies who underbid the now bankrupt American tool and die shops in the first place.

Make Sure You Have The Cash For A Long Battle – Most new companies do not show a profit for the first five years of their existence. That's a long time to work for nothing. Add to that the stress it will cause on you and your family, and you begin to get an understanding of the real costs involved. Disregard everything the Ivy League tells you, and make sure you have at least twice as much money as you need to get to the finish line when running a new business.

NIGHTMARE BUSINESSES

Going into business the conventional way is a nightmare. If you are going to do it, you may as well optimize your chances for success by employing the successful business practices of some of history's most cutthroat businessmen.

Stay the hell away from the following businesses—they have astronomical failure rates, and will cause you more mental problems than any dozen drug-toting psychiatrists can cure:

Restaurants – Four out of five restaurants fail in the first five years. It's backbreaking work, and causes more divorces than good-looking deliverymen.

Video Rental Stores – The new video-on-demand services being implemented by the major cable and satellite companies are about to drive most of these stores into extinction.

Mom and Pop Retail Stores – Big retail fish always eat little retail fish; make no mistake about it. Open up a new store of some sort, and it is highly likely that one of the retail giants will stick their boot so far up your shorts, you'll need a gurney to get you to bankruptcy court.

The Furniture Business – Not a week goes by when you don't hear about some unemployed carpenter who decided to open up a furniture business because he or she is good with their hands. Let me tell you everything you need to know about the furniture business—most sofas, tables, chairs, cabinets, beds, etc., are now made offshore somewhere by prison laborers earning two coconuts a week. You simply cannot compete with those labor costs.

Internet Pornography – Every unemployed genius you run into is convinced they can still make a killing by starting a porno web site. False assumption. There are now so many adult web sites offering free nude pictures and movies, it is become extremely difficult for anyone to make any money selling pictures of their ex-girlfriend on the net.

800 Number Sex Talk Business – Stay away from these. While they were once all the rage, they are now very ubiquitous. If you pick up the phone and use a service like this, you're apt to encounter an out of work relative on the other end of the line pretending to be a bowlegged cheerleader.

Mobile Automotive Oil Change Service – Every moronic business magazine in the world tries to convince you that this is a great idea that has never been done before, and you should invest your severance pay immediately. Not a month goes by that you don't hear about some guy who tries this, and then gets pinned under a car that has fallen off the jack stand.

Hip Hop / Rap / Karaoke D.J. For Rent – The minute Eminem made his fortune, everyone in America decided they could go into the D.J. business and work the wedding / bar / strip club / bar mitzvah / corporate event circuit. The problem with most of these people is an absence of talent. You can only hop around the stage in baggy pants for so long before people start noticing that you have no talent, and pull out their guns and start shooting.

Auto Restoration Business – The market for restored automobiles is fairly small, yet countless mechanics and handymen go into this business each year convinced they are going to find an old Bugatti in the basement of some hillbilly's house, restore it, and make a million bucks. This is the same mentality that believes that if they buy a metal detector and walk the beach long enough, they'll find a rare coin and retire rich. It is not going to happen. You'll find plenty of used condoms and a couple hundred empty beer cans, but no rare coin and no Bugatti.

An Internet Business – This is the mother of all myths. For some reason, five minutes after most people lose their jobs they decide they have a great Internet money-making idea. They buy or build their own web site and then, contrary to what they've been told, nothing happens.

Criminal Business Model Gangsters view self-employment as a birthright. They view working for someone else as a slow death that is to be avoided at all costs.

GangsterNomic Legitimate Business Model Alternative Use self-employment as a vehicle to exploit and capitalize upon whatever you have learned from previous employers, partners and associates.

GANGSTERNOMIC MANAGEMENT

If you are going to manage a business, there are some things you need to understand about proper GangsterNomic management tools. Whether you're running a criminal enterprise or a Fortune 500 company is really irrelevant because, in this day and age, the management techniques are essentially the same.

First, you have to throw out all the warm and fuzzy politically correct managerial theories you were taught in business school. They may have sounded good on paper, but the real world of business is far too ugly, competitive and treacherous to tolerate such simplistic answers.

The First Rule Of GangsterNomic Management - All employees, managers and high-level executives are completely expendable and replaceable.

The Second Rule Of GangsterNomic Management – All employees, managers and high-level executives should be compelled to perpetually compete for their own jobs, with new recruits offering greater skill sets and revenue generating ability.

The Third Rule Of GangsterNomic Management
Terminate any subordinate whose superior abilities and
experience threaten your own job security.

The Fourth Rule Of GangsterNomic Management - Less
attractive employees tend to be smarter and harder
working than more attractive employees. They also tend to
file fewer sexual harassment suits.

The Fifth Rule Of GangsterNomic Management – Balls
and persistence are far more important than IQ when it
comes to sales. You are much better off with a guy or girl
who is extremely determined and full of fire, than you will
be with an MBA who will over-analyze every move he
makes to the point of paralysis.

The Sixth Rule Of GangsterNomic Management - Hiring
foreign and offshore workers is now a standard component
of most business plans. If you need creative, legal or
managerial genius, think domestic. If you are simply
looking for extremely low hourly labor rates on
conventional or professional labor, then think offshore.

The Seventh Rule Of GangsterNomic Management - All
employees will try to exploit you sooner or later. Given that,
it is important to protect yourself with employment and
confidentiality contracts.

The Eighth Rule Of GangsterNomic Management
Expect hard work but reward innovation. Working hard is
now an absolute minimal prerequisite for retaining a job,
but being innovative is an employee trait that all managers
should look for on their evaluation radar screens.

The Ninth Rule Of GangsterNomic Management - Once
a pain, always a pain. Terminate any employee that
appears as though the problems they cause will only
continue to escalate.

The Tenth Rule Of GangsterNomic Management
Always try to hire people on salary instead of hourly. This way you can compel them to work horrific amounts of overtime without paying them for it.

The Eleventh Rule Of GangsterNomic Management
When hiring people from a competitor, always target those individuals who made the greatest contribution to that company's success.

The Twelth Rule Of GangsterNomic Management
Whenever firing someone, always try to have a subordinate do the actual firing. Hopefully this will minimize the likelihood of any ill will or hostility being directed at you personally.

The Thirteenth Rule Of GangsterNomic Management
Never date or socialize with subordinates—It tends to fuel the litigation flames when things eventually go south.

The Fourteenth Rule Of GangsterNomic Management
Always blame your company's or division's poor performance on the subordinate who is least likely to sue you when you blame them.

The Fifteenth Rule Of GangsterNomic Management
Always try to take as much credit as possible for any positive accomplishment or innovation your subordinate comes up with.

The Sixteenth Rule Of GangsterNomic Management
Use video, electronic and computer surveillance as much as possible to help keep employee theft to a minimum.

The Seventeenth Rule Of GangsterNomic Management
Do not be reluctant to hire older workers just because you think they will be more expensive. The fact of the matter is, older workers tend to have a superior work ethic, more experience, and tend to party less.

The Eighteenth Rule Of GangsterNomic Management
When possible, try to find a replacement before firing someone. This not only eases the transition, but also keep productivity higher.

The Nineteenth Rule Of GangsterNomic Management
Always be positive; respectful yet firm. Show any signs of weakness whatsoever, and employees will tend to take advantage of that.

The Twentieth Rule Of GangsterNomic Management
Eventually, the company will attempt to apply one of the above rules to you in an effort to force you out. When that happens, go into business for yourself and give your former employer a run for their money.

OCCULT-DRIVEN MANAGEMENT

There are countless media reports of world leaders (from former U.S. presidents to Central American dictators), who have made exhaustive use of psychics and astrologers when planning their next strategic move.

The practice is even more popular in the world of organized crime. Whether it's Caribbean drug dealers or South American drug cartels, the ingenuity is always impressive. Some will even use Internet video conferencing with psychics and astrologers from all points of the globe to try to minimize their risks, and get a sense of how perilous their next deal will really be.

The reason so many people in power are inclined to use psychic sources is because when it works, it works extremely well. As a producer, I can tell you that I've had occasion to work with clairvoyants in the past. Ninety-nine percent of them are either complete frauds or just incompetent. The remaining one percent can, and often will, provide people with information that can make them wealthy, save their lives, or most importantly for some, keep them out of jail.

When compared to other forms of intelligence gathering, gifted clairvoyants are by far the most cost-effective.

DEALING WITH A GANGSTERNOMIC MANAGER

There is a growing ruthlessness in the way managers have been treating employees in today's workplace. It is fueling a perpetual sense of hostility, resulting in escalating workplace violence.

Many of these circumstances are the result of the tremendous loss of leverage workers have experienced over the last few decades. The more jobs that are sent overseas, the less secure workers feel, and the more empowered management becomes in exploiting that insecurity.

Below are some things you can do to preserve your rights and strengthen your position.

The single most important thing you can do to increase your job security is to maximize your productivity. If the layoffs come, they tend to hit the less productive employees first.

The second thing you can do if your job does becomes vulnerable is to begin checking with other departments in your company to see if there are any openings.

The final, and perhaps most important thing to consider, is to maintain a perpetual job search. It never hurts to seek out other employment options, even if things are going well. Just be very careful responding to blind job postings, as they may have been placed by your own employer. Having your employer find out that you are job searching by accidentally sending him your resume is a great way to compromise your current position, and will sometimes even result in your dismissal.

Criminal Business Model *The ruthless treatment of subordinates in the world of organized crime has been a long-established tradition designed to maintain fear and order.*

GangsterNomic Legitimate Business Model Alternative *The ruthless treatment of subordinates and employees in the corporate world is now so firmly entrenched in so many companies that the very nature of most workplaces has become perpetually adversarial.*

DESPERATION MANAGEMENT TACTICS

You can always tell when a company or criminal organization is desperate because their managerial decision-making takes on an air of impetuous recklessness.

With criminal entities you will often see a rapid escalation of violence where negotiation would have been used previously. You will also see a manic reshuffling of the senior guard as people are killed or simply disappear.

In corporations, the signs are usually apparent in the moves below:

Sales Force Reorganization – Panic-stricken or unfocused vice presidents will begin by blaming the sales force for their problems. This usually means doing the "commission two-step." If the sales people are on commission they will be taken off and put on salary. If they're on salary then they will be put on commission. The end result often means little or no difference to the bottom line. This sort of move is usually driven by uninspired thinking.

Merger Separation Two-Step – This is another small-minded move often embarked on by new vice presidents who think tactically rather than strategically. If most of the corporation's divisions operate autonomously, then the new manager will usually unite them under a single vice president tasked with finding new efficiencies that can be extracted from this consolidation. If most of the divisions operate under a single flag, then the new vice president will come in and proclaim that they need more autonomy so that they can pursue goals and opportunities more efficiently. Either move tends to make little difference.

Acquisition Rampage – When cash-rich companies run out of foolish ideas, they usually start acquiring at a feverish pace. A few highly targeted acquisitions make sense but the vast majority do not. There are circumstances when acquiring another company is the right move because it lowers costs or provides an access to technology or markets. This is rare, though. As demonstrated over the last three decades, statistically speaking most acquisitions make no business sense whatsoever. Most of them were driven by pure ego, something both male and female CEOs tend to be overly endowed with. Other acquisitions are simply a function of having too much set aside in cash reserves. In the end, most acquisitions result in the accumulation of so much new debt, it eventually slows or reverses any financial progress the company may have been making.

Relocating Too Many Resources Overseas – There is an invisible, and often difficult to define, threshold that should not be crossed by companies who move their employees and assets overseas. It is the point at which a company has moved so many of its employees, factories or technology offshore, it has become inordinately vulnerable to political peril and economic risk. Not the everyday risk that one assumes when operating a business, but the sort of problem that comes flying out of nowhere, hits you where you're most vulnerable, and then makes headlines.

Ignoring Executive Flight – This one screams five-alarm corporate fire. Whenever an unusually high percentage of senior management resigns within a short time frame, it always means trouble. If it is ignored, downplayed or denied, then it usually means the CEO has gone off the tracks, the company is sinking financially, the board of directors has been undermined, or someone is about to be indicted. Another thing you can count on: the more the company denies that there's a problem, the bigger that problem really is. Mass executive flight is very problematic.

Hyper Inflated Advertising Budgets – Whenever sales head south or the product line is lackluster, inept managers will pour vast sums of money into advertising to try and blind consumers or create a false sense of momentum. This dated technique used to work in the short run, but with the advent of the Internet, word of a product's poor performance spreads so quickly that this approach is now a huge waste of money.

Spinning Off Under-Performing Subsidiaries – Whenever a company initiates a sequence of sell-offs designed to rid it of under-performing subsidiaries, it is usually a tacit acknowledgement of senior management's own incompetence or lack of imagination. What they are really saying is that no one here is smart enough or creative enough to fix this problem, so let's sell it to someone that is.

Hyper-Inflated Executive Salaries And Bonuses – Whenever senior management attempts to negotiate or collect salaries, bonuses or stock options that are so substantial they could feed third world nations, it is usually very ominous. They will always make the same tired old argument..."If I create X amount of wealth, then I should be able to share in a reasonable percentage of that wealth." The problem with this self-serving logic is in the interpretation of the word "reasonable". The problem is, most companies will get hit with a shareholder lawsuit down the road when the stock price starts to decline. The suit almost always claims malfeasance on the part of the board of directors, and insists on the disgorgement of what the plaintiff stockholders will inevitably characterize as unreasonably high salaries and bonuses.

Managerial desperation is something that is becoming more common than ever before. It is extremely well-concealed these days by public relations departments, but if you look for some of the clues mentioned above you can usually detect them.

THE MOST PROFITABLE CULINARY ART—COOKING THE BOOKS

The one GangsterNomic area of commerce that both organized crime and the corporate sector share is a unique love of accounting. No other business model or practice on the face of the earth has generated more profit for organized crime, or corporate America, than the practice of accounting.

Not conventional accounting, mind you, but rather a subspecialty of it. It is the type of accounting which allows some Fortune 500 firms trading on the New York Stock Exchange to appear to be generating billions of dollars in profit, when in reality they're up to their retinas in the kind of debt that would sink most third world countries.

It is the kind of accounting that auditors like to call "aggressive", and criminals like to characterize as business as usual.

Minute by minute, hour by hour, there is no other activity that generates more money for the effort than "cooking the books".

Whether it happens in organized crime, a seemingly legitimate Fortune 500 company, or within a government office, there is no better way to make money.

Cooking the books is also an activity that is governed by the "Law Of Big Lies". This law states that "The More Epic The Deception, The Less Likely It Is To Be Questioned". That is why, in many jurisdictions, the criminal penalty for stealing five billion dollars is not much harsher than the sentencing guideline for stealing five hundred dollars. Think about the GangsterNomic message that this sends.

BUSINESSES WITH MORE ECONOMIC POTENTIAL THAN SELLING DRUGS

Here are ten businesses you can give serious consideration to, without worrying about foreign competition, inflation or interest rates:

Church Of Any Denomination – What a great business. If I had the time I would open a half a dozen churches tomorrow. I would hire some motivational speakers who just got out of rehab and let them have at it. I'd locate the churches in abandoned nightclubs, liquor stores and car washes. I would charge an extra five dollars to have a preacher bless you as you're having your car detailed. Throw in another ten bucks and I'll have a bishop hop out of the closet and forgive you for all your sins while you're getting your wheels waxed. Do you know there are mega churches in the United States now that have their own hip hop recording studios, TV broadcast centers and clothing lines? There is no end to the possibilities. You could set up a mobile church confessional in front of every strip club in America and charge a dollar to forgive peoples' sins while they're waiting for the valet to bring their car. I love this business.

Temporary Employment Agency – This is another business with no limit in demand. Every time a new industry pops up, there is a new batch of temp agencies that cater to it. Want to hire an Asian programmer? There's a temp agency just for that. What about a home care worker? Same thing. There are even agencies that can help you find a reputable dog walker.

Discount Funeral Home – Have you priced out a modest funeral these days? There's no such thing. I am convinced that the cost of funerals will soon exceed the economic reach of the average middle class family. The funeral industry is fairly confident in the ability of its lobbyists to keep prices inflated, but it is only a matter of time before a very aggressive discounter moves into the marketplace and lets you bury someone for about two hundred dollars.

Check Cashing Service – This industry is growing very rapidly. According to the U.S. Treasury, approximately ten percent of American households have no bank account. A growing number of these places will also loan you money against the title of your car. These short term and micro-loan businesses are becoming de facto banking institutions in neighborhoods where people cannot even afford cable TV.

Automotive Repair Service – Have you noticed that Toyota has moved into second place amongst car manufacturers? It's because their vehicles continue to run flawlessly long after the warranty expires. Have you driven a car that's made by some of the other manufacturers lately? They tend to break down several times a year at a considerable expense. Domestic automotive dealers now routinely look you in the eye with a straight face and charge you a hundred dollars an hour or more to repair your car. In many cases, it would be less expensive to have a team of lawyers fix it. A heavily discounted and reputable automotive repair center would do tremendous volumes in the right neighborhoods.

Liquor Store – Drive through any urban area and you will notice no shortage of liquor stores. Most of them are family-operated. Many of them have expanded to include cell phone shops, delis and even baked goods. There seems to be no limit to what people will buy when they're in the mood to get drunk.

Car Wash – Here is another all-cash business that seems to thrive no matter what, if the price point is low enough. Charge $2 to $3 and they'll line up down the block when the sun comes out.

Coin Operated Laundry – This one continues to do well across a wide variety of demographics and zip codes for all the obvious reasons. I marvel at the fact that someone has not combined the laundry business with a coffee shop or bookstore. One spends similar amounts of time in each.

Topless Nightclub – This is the GangsterNomic Mecca of business opportunities. With Fortune 500 companies getting into mainstream pornography, it is only a matter of time before Wall Street finances the rollout of a high-end national topless nightclub chain. If you can do it without your wife divorcing you, then in most marketplaces, this opportunity still presents all kinds of possibilities.

Movie Theater Day Care Center – Parents are always strapped for a babysitter when it's time to go see a movie or get a bite to eat. Opening up a day care center at or near a mall with a major movie theater complex would be a natural fit and great synergy.

Criminal Business Model Gangsters never view operating a business as a long-term endeavor. It is always seen by them as a vehicle for getting to the next level, which is usually a larger or more lucrative business.

GangsterNomic Legitimate Business Model Alternative Choose the type of business you enter based on qualities that are not as apparent to others. Look for reversible adversity or exploitable opportunity.

ETHNIC SHOPPING MALLS AND
RESTAURANT PLAZAS

American communities used to be fairly unique. Now, as you drive from coast to coast you get the growing impression that the entire country has become one large shopping mall. You tend to see the same chain stores and restaurants on every corner of every strip mall.

As innovation is one of the principal driving forces behind GangsterNomics, I would like to see a little more diversity. One option worthy of consideration would be the construction of Ethnocentric Shopping Malls and Restaurant Plazas.

In overly-developed areas I think that shopping malls and restaurant plazas comprised of stores and restaurants from a multitude of nations would be both unique and highly popular. If you think about it, when was the last time you saw anyone in the U.S. open a strip mall without the same old stores you see everywhere else?

FRANCHISES—ARE YOU KIDDING ME?

The number of franchise business opportunities seems to double every few years. There is no end to it. Each of them operates under a similar model: "pay us "X" number of dollars and we'll show you how to run one of our businesses. Pay us even more money, and we'll set up a business for you and help you run it."

The selling feature of franchises is that they have all the systems in place to help you succeed. They claim to help you pick out a location, set up the physical layout, provide inventory, accounting and marketing. But if you cast a GangsterNomic eye on this opportunity and review it carefully, you will notice a number of problems:

1) The franchise company will control every aspect of your business and its operation. Many of them will reserve the right to come in and shut you down if you deviate in any way from their system.

2) Many of them will require a five-figure deposit just to put you on a waiting list that is several years long.

3) You will assume all the financial risk of opening up the place.

4) The franchise company will take a considerable portion of your weekly gross as its franchise fee.

5) If some franchise operator in another state mismanages his business and generates a great deal of negative press, it will also affect you adversely. Just as good news about a national franchise helps everyone, bad news hurts everyone.

Under some limited set of circumstances it might make sense to get a franchise, but if you're a GangsterNomic businessperson interested in making serious money, then you should do so on your own. There is no need to have a major corporation's hands around your throat while you struggle to make them money. Do it on your own.

THE HORROR AND BEAUTY OF NIGHTCLUB OWNERSHIP

Nightclubs are one of those businesses that have created more fortunes, driven more people into bankruptcy, and caused more marriages and divorces than just about any other industry I can think of. All that aside, what is really interesting about the nightclub business is the differences in management styles between the clubs run by gangsters, and those run by straight businessmen.

I see it all the time. Whenever a guy makes some serious money, a bulb goes off over his head and he decides he'd like to open a nightclub.

Regardless of what industry made them rich, they invariably dream about owning their own bar. In the eighties, they wanted to run a disco. In the nineties, it was sports bars. Today, it's pretty much anything. You name it—it's out there. Theme bars, gay bars, coffee bars, oxygen bars, topless bars, dance bars, sushi bars, and country and western joints. Regardless of who is involved, bars are all making or losing someone lots of money.

The beauty of GangsterNomics is that it provides you with a glimpse into what is really going on behind the economic façade. So, without any further adieu, I'm going to pull the curtain back and give you a rare glimpse into the nightclub business.

The first thing you need to know about the nightclub business is that a significant percentage of them are operated purely for money laundering purposes. No one even talks about it any more, because it is one of the worst-kept secrets in the business world.

You see them everywhere—clubs that do well on a Saturday night, but are almost empty the other six nights. Some of them don't even do that well on the weekend. A number of these clubs are owned by gangsters who need a legitimate place to launder their money, and nothing washes cash like a nightclub.

What is truly entertaining is when a legitimate businessman decides to open up a club on the same street as one of these money laundering clubs. The straightlaced guy will dump a ton of money into his club and its promotion, and then sit back and watch it slowly fade. He looks down the street and sees his competitor remodeling his place every eighteen months and thinks maybe that's the key. He dumps another fortune into the remodeling of his club, and the same thing happens. Things go well for a couple of months, and then they just fade away again.

Eventually, the legit bar owner will toss his hands into the air and curse the day he got into the club business. The place closes and he moves on. What he didn't realize is that it is very difficult to compete with a club that doesn't really need to generate money. In fact, it's almost impossible.

Another brutal reality of the nightclub business is that they are extremely subject to pop culture trends and changes in taste, and that is one of the reasons the clubs get remodeled as often as they do. The marketplace is constantly changing.

I know a nightclub in the Midwest that has been remodeled five times in twelve years, and has gone through three owners during the same period. Its business cycle is so predictable you can almost map it out. First, there is a major remodeling of the club, followed by the announcement of a grand opening date, which will be hosted and promoted by a local radio station.

The club opens and does well for about six months, and then things begin to slow down so management brings in a few new promoters to try and stir up some business. This works for a while until it too begins to fade.

Then management decides that they need to launch a new radio campaign to drum up more business, so they pour money into that for a while. It causes a short-term spike, but not enough to warrant the ongoing expense of buying radio airtime. At this point one of two things will happen. They will decide to remodel, or they will padlock the doors and sell. This cycle just goes on and on.

Years ago, there were a number of nightclubs that thought it would be fun and profitable to put real phones at each table (this was before cell phones). The idea was to get people to come to the bar and interact by calling each other's tables; supposedly this would help people overcome their shyness. The phones made it possible for you to ask a girl to dance without having to actually walk across the entire bar to face possible rejection. If she said no, you've been spared the embarrassment of walking over to her and being blown off in front of your friends. It was a pretty innovative idea, but it didn't really last that long. My point is that the popularity cycle amongst bars are short and getting shorter. This will dramatically impact your ability to generate long-term profits.

Most men go into the nightclub business thinking it will be a great way to meet women. It's true if you are single, and even more so if you're married. Just don't make it your principal reason for embarking on the venture.

Another interesting dissimilarity between legitimate bar owners and the other guys is their choice of locations. The straight guys will usually try to open a bar in the nicest part of town, while gangsters will go into the ghetto and remodel some hellhole of a building and turn it into a raging dance club. The irony is that for the first six months of its business cycle, the clubs that opened in the worst parts of town tended to do much better than clubs in the suburbs.

Another major myth amongst aspiring bar owners is the belief that owning a club will be a great way to generate cash, which you can squirrel away and avoid paying any taxes on. That may have been true years ago, but now many bar tabs are paid with credit cards, so not much of your income will be from cash.

Another problem with dance clubs and bars in general is that fights tend to break out on a regular basis. In the old days, the bouncers would just grab the troublemakers, toss them out the door, and let the police have their way with them. Today, municipalities are fed up with the expense and liability of having to pay the overtime necessary to police bars with unruly histories, so they've passed the "Five And You're Out" ordinance. These laws vary from city to city, but they basically all state the same thing. If the police department has to come to your bar more than "X" number of times over an "X" period of time, then your license will suspended or revoked.

This is a serious problem for bar owners because it is not one they can fully control. Some establishments have responded to this by hiring more bouncers than they need. The idea is to intimidate the crowd and keep them calm before a fight breaks out.

TOPLESS BARS AND MENTAL INSTITUTES

Two of the worst kept secrets in the business world are 1) topless bars are tremendous cash cows, and 2) many topless bars are either owned or controlled by organized crime.

What is interesting is that corporate America and Wall Street are now viewing topless bars with the same "cash envy" they had back in the seventies and eighties when they saw what was going on in Vegas. Back then, they saw how much money organized crime was taking out of the desert, so they decided to pour billions of junk bond dollars into the city to erect some of the largest casinos the world has ever seen.

Now the experts on Wall Street are analyzing the success of the topless bar industry, and they're no doubt going to be thinking the following:

How much would it cost to finance the rollout of a national, high-end, gentleman's topless bar chain?

How long can we afford to delay doing this before some other conglomerate beats us to the market?

With many topless dancers averaging between $500 and $5000 per night, how can we employ our tremendous labor cost reduction skills to redirect more of that lap dance money into the corporation's pockets?

How can we develop a topless bar brand image that will be both unique and highly appealing to the marketplace?

The answers to all these questions are very simple. The cost of a national topless bar rollout would be fairly nominal. One could establish a new high-end club in twenty-five of the largest markets for about 125 million dollars. Those clubs will then easily generate 100 million dollars per year.

You could initiate a very clever and comedic advertising campaign which positioned these new high-end clubs as "mental institutes" and "spas" designed to help patrons cope with the stresses of everyday life by receiving treatment from the expertly-trained medical staff of dancers.

One could even take things a step further and create hybrid topless clubs. On one level, it would be a conventional topless bar where clients paid to watch dancers, and on another floor, there would be the actual nightclub where people gathered to drink and dance with each other. The uniqueness and synergy generated by the combination of the two would make it very hard for traditional clubs to compete.

The corporations could then create a Stripper Satellite Network which would broadcast twenty-four hours a day out of each of the clubs. It would provide tremendous publicity, and generate another revenue stream.

Wall Street has lost any reluctance they may once have had to entering industries which may be deemed by some to be immoral. Major conglomerates trading on the New York Stock Exchange have already invested very heavily in cable and satellite pornography, adult publishing, casinos, arms and munitions, and even hospitals that practice abortion. It is only a matter of time before someone writes the check necessary to roll out a high-end national topless bar chain. When this happens, the financial success they realize will cause countless others to follow.

Criminal Business Model *Organized crime has operated many topless bars across the country essentially as sole proprietorships.*

GangsterNomic Legitimate Business Model Alternative *It is only a matter of time before a major conglomerate rolls out a national chain of high-end topless bars. They will apply highly sophisticated business models, marketing techniques and technology to make the chain a tremendous nationwide moneymaker. It is also very probable that they will employ aggressive cost-cutting measures to see to it that much of the $500 to $5000 per night made by the dancers ends up in their corporate coffers.*

PROFITING FROM THE COLLAPSE OF THE REAL ESTATE MARKET

Organized crime does not invest in real estate for the same reasons other people do. For most criminal enterprises, real estate is nothing more than an opportunity to conceal or launder money.

Back in the eighties when rivers of cocaine were flowing through south Florida, there was a tremendous boom in the number of skyscrapers and commercial buildings built in the Miami area. This was not a coincidence. Many of those buildings were erected with narco-dollars that were laundered very effectively when they were poured into those towers.

As far as most criminals are concerned, real estate has always had the added benefit of appreciating over time, which meant they could usually expect a modest return on their investment; not the ten thousand percent profit you might expect on a suitcase full of drugs, but a respectable profit nonetheless. Real estate also provides a certain emotional comfort to people who work in an industry were every day just may be their last.

In my opinion, North American real estate has already begun what can best be described as a slow motion implosion. In listening to the experts discussing the probability of the real estate bubble bursting, most of them are analyzing it using references that date back over the last century.

You will hear the same theories over and over. The print and media experts will say that if the bubble does burst and you hold onto to your real estate investment, it will eventually recover. They will then provide the standard examples of past boom/bust cycles, which eventually reversed themselves as the next bullish market began. Interest rates adjusted, the economy came back, and the real estate market got hot again.

That is not going to happen this time.

When the bubble bursts, there will be no reversal in either the short term or foreseeable future. You will see all sorts of machinations attempted, but the result will be ineffective. The reason is that too many subsistence-level American jobs are being exported offshore, which is reducing the number of qualified homebuyers as well as eroding the confidence of those still working.

Previous recessions were usually followed by a turnaround in the economy, which sent people back to work. As folks started working again, the real estate market re-ignited and fueled the economy's growth.

The problem today is that it's not only the jobs that are being sent overseas, but the capital equipment as well. Every time a plant shuts down in the U.S., special brokers fly in from Asia and other parts of the world to acquire that plant's dies, equipment and manufacturing machinery for pennies on the dollar. It is then shipped overseas to new factories set up to exploit low wage labor.

If the President of the United States and Congress suddenly passed a law forbidding the offshoring of any more jobs effective immediately, it would not make much difference because our manufacturing base has been gutted.

The signs of this collapsing real estate market are everywhere. Banks and mortgage companies are pushing interest-only and forty-year mortgages with very aggressive ad campaigns. Despite low rates for quite some time now, the length of time a property is listed before selling has increased ten-fold in some marketplaces.

Here is another sign the experts won't talk about, because doing so would only increase the chances of the market slowdown occurring:

The average number of household occupants per urban home has gone up significantly. Don't look at the official statistics to confirm this because those are designed to portray as positive an image as possible.

Talk to realtors and landlords who are your friends. Ask them if they have noticed a dramatic increase in the number of people occupying homes in the city. If they are honest with you they will confirm this. In the old days, if you rented out a home to a couple of folks, you would put their names on the lease because that's who was supposed to live there. Today, if you rent a home to two people and return in a month to pay them a surprise Sunday morning visit, you're likely to find six to twelve occupants sharing the home. You see this a lot in communities which are affected by a heavy influx of illegal aliens. It is also a growing phenomenon in cities which have recently experienced a number of major plant closings.

Looking overseas, you will see enormous low-income shantytowns in which tens of thousands of people live in cardboard boxes or metal shacks. What you see in American inner cities now are the very earliest stages of this same phenomenon—only with homeless Americans, it begins with shopping carts rather than metal shacks

What can be done to mitigate the effect of all this on you, as well as allow you to profit from it? Here are a number of GangsterNomic suggestions:

Exotic Superhomes – Of all the expensive homes on the market, the exotic and overly eccentric high-end homes will take the biggest plunge in market value. Mansions with unconventional architecture and overly trendy layouts will see their market value plunge by as much as 80% in the first year. Many of these homes will become virtually unsalable, as buyers in this price range tend to build to their own exact tastes and specifications. For many of these homes, the only value remaining will be in the land they sit on. If you own a home in this category, you may wish to consider putting it on the market yesterday.

High Income Homes – When the real estate meltdown begins to occur, it will hit this sector very hard. You will see fifteen million dollars homes lose two thirds of their value in a year. Million dollar homes will lose about half their value in that same period, and will take much longer to sell. If you reside in a home in this price range, you should consider having your attorney take very aggressive action to convince your municipality that your property taxes should decrease by a commensurate amount. Something many people in this price range may wish to consider is immediately selling their home to someone willing to rent it back to them. This way you can cash out and let your home's declining valuation hit someone else's portfolio.

When the meltdown hits bottom you can then offer to reacquire your home (or an even larger one) for thirty cents on the dollar.

Waterfront Property – Unlike high-income homes which reside in conventional areas, waterfront property will retain more of its value during the meltdown. While most high-end homes will lose as much as two thirds of their value, waterfront property shouldn't take more than a fifty percent hit—the reason being that owners of waterfront homes tend to have a stronger emotional attachment to them than owners of non-waterfront property, and are therefore less likely to put them up for sale. This reluctance to list will limit the supply and thus minimize their overall decline in value.

Commercial Property – The downward trend of the real estate market will dramatically affect the rest of the economy. When this happens, I predict that commercial real estate will take a major hit. As the situation worsens and the market is flooded with listings, it will be very difficult for banks and lenders to foreclose on all these properties and somehow salvage their investment. If anything, banks will be more inclined to renegotiate their outstanding mortgages, and hope that the people managing these commercial properties can stay afloat long enough to turn things around.

Midlevel Homes – Homes in the $125,000 to $600,000 price range will also take a major drop in value. Since this is such a large sector of the marketplace, many of these owners will stay in their homes as long as possible. Those that are eventually forced to walk away will encounter a bank that is very eager to renegotiate the mortgage rather than lose them entirely and have the property sit vacant.

Starter Homes And Condos – Those units which are under $125,000 will retain the most marketability, but will still have to deal with much longer listing periods. The most desirable of these homes will be those that can accommodate a larger family or group of families. That means having more bathrooms, finished basements with extra bedrooms, and whenever possible, separate entrances and utilities. Homes that can serve as unofficial multiple dwellings for several families will have the greatest market value and shortest turnaround time.

Trailer Parks – When the meltdown occurs, you will see an explosion in the growth of trailer park communities. With some previously owned trailers costing less than a used car, this will become one of the few hot growth sectors in the real estate market.

If you are thinking about capitalizing on this situation, then here are some opportunities to think about:

Foreign Real Estate – Today homes in countries like Hungary, Czech Republic, Mexico, Romania and the Ukraine can be purchased or built for a fraction of what they cost in the United States. When these markets take off, you will start to see 100% to 150% annualized rates of appreciation. Just a few decades ago, you could build a beautiful three story brick home in Poland for less than $5000. Today their home prices are comparable to what is being seen in the U.S. This same scenario will eventually begin to unfold in countries like Hungary, Romania and the Ukraine. If the North American real estate meltdown should ever take on global proportions, then the values of homes in these countries really will not have much downside exposure since they are already so low.

Multi-Dwelling Properties – As the economic consolidation continues in the real estate market, more families and groups of people will be cohabiting than ever seen before. This pattern will sustain a healthy demand for low-income multi-dwelling homes, apartment buildings and condos. Acquiring or building property like this should allow you to generate a very healthy rental income stream for quite some time.

Inner City Renovations – Run-down homes in urban centers will take on new potential as the free-falling real estate market will cause people to look with renewed favor upon rental property in the cities. While you will have to assume additional risks in these areas, you will also be able to tap into a huge market of ex-suburbanites who have been forced to move to something more affordable in the inner city. Another nice characteristic of these neighborhoods is that they contain a large percentage of multi-family properties that can be rented out at a profit from day one.

Single To MultiDwelling Conversions – Another tremendous investment opportunity will be created by converting single family units to multi-family units. As more family, friends and roommates are forced to live together for economic reasons, the demand for multi-unit homes will grow dramatically. When this occurs, companies that specialize in converting single family homes into multi-family dwellings will do extremely well, by adding separate entrances, additional bathrooms and bedrooms, finished basements and separate utility meters. A conversion like this will not only increase the rental income potential of the property, but it will also increase its resale potential.

The problem with all of this is that, if the real estate meltdown is severe enough, it will have a very damaging effect on the economy. That is why it's very important to make certain that your portfolio is not too heavily invested in real estate.

Of all the properties that will begin to rapidly depreciate, those located on or near the water in warmer climates will probably lose the least value over time. Being located on fresh water is always more desirable than being located near a salt-water body. Homes with ocean views have always commanded huge premiums, but the recent tsunami and hurricane events have made insuring them economically more difficult.

Insurance Issues – Another consideration is the insurability of your investment. Over the last few years, many insurance companies have increased their premiums so aggressively that I predict the real estate meltdown will be accompanied by a record number of homeowners canceling their insurance. At first, the banks and mortgage companies will object fiercely and impose penalties, fines and even their own insurance. When a growing number of homeowners simply become unable to make those insurance payments, then either the Federal government will intervene, or you will witness a wholesale downward adjustment of insurance rates.

In Japan, they have managed to sustain the insanity of hyper-inflated real estate prices by offering one-hundred-year mortgages which are passed down from one generation to the next. The viability of implementing something like that in the United States is a little questionable in that most Americans would be very reluctant to pass their debt down to their children.

PHANTOM MORTGAGES FOR STOLEN HOMES

Over the last few years, the home mortgage industry has been victimized by a growing number of mortgage companies involved in so much illegal activity, it is causing an unprecedented number of homeowners to lose their property.

The scams are almost too numerous to count, but many of them revolve around the same basic techniques. They usually involve falsified quitclaim deeds, hyper-inflated appraisals, altered income documents, and adjustable interest rate mortgages that increase so dramatically they force the homeowner into default.

There are three main categories of mortgage scams. The first is designed to perform a refinance which allows you to fraudulently take cash out of a home you do not own. The second category of scams are designed to refinance homes for people in a manner deliberately intended to cause them to default so that the lender can later seize their property for pennies on the dollar. The third group of scams is designed to help people obtain mortgages who do not qualify for them.

The net result of all this mortgage fraud is the creation of a lending marketplace in which it is becoming increasingly difficult to tell the difference between legitimate mortgage companies and those that operate outside the law.

Criminal Business Model *Fraudulent mortgage activity designed to steal peoples' homes or take cash out of property belonging to someone else has reached an unprecedented level.*

GangsterNomic Legitimate Business Model Alternative *Whenever possible, try to secure your mortgage with an established bank or mortgage company that has a long history of reputability in the community, and has been referred to you by someone you trust. Try not to purchase a second home before you sell your first. The minute your mortgage company hears that you have the tremendous pressure of both a sale and a purchase pending, they will use this to their advantage by ambushing you at the closing table with a higher interest rate. They'll do this because they know it is highly improbable that you will walk away and ruin two deals. If possible, stay away from interest-only mortgages. They will put you in a perpetual state of debt without ever allowing you to accumulate any real equity. The lender will bait you by telling you that you'll be able to refinance again in a few years and get a conventional mortgage, but that is highly unlikely given peoples' propensity to accumulate even more debt as they get older. That just makes it harder for them to qualify.*

VENTURE CAPITAL ACQUISITION
GANGSTERNOMIC STYLE

Acquiring venture capital for a new business or technology can be almost as difficult as locating financing for a new movie or television show. Below is a list of what are, in my opinion, some of the best and most respected venture capital (VC) firms:

Benchmark Capital
Kleiner, Perkins, Caufield & Byers
Sequoia Capital
Norwest Venture Partners
Sutter Hill Ventures
Bessemer Venture Partners
Venrock Associates
Redpoint Ventures
New Enterprise Associates
Accel Partners
US Venture Partners
Vulcan Ventures
Lightspeed Venture Partners
Crosspoint Venture Partners
General Atlantic Partners

For obvious reasons many VC firms are located in Silicon Valley. If you visit their web sites, you will find sections explaining how to apply for venture capital. Here are some things you should know before you embark on this process:

Venture capital acquisition is a phenomenon that is very trend-directed. It bears a resemblance to the entertainment industry and the decision-making process it goes through when deciding which film or TV project to finance. Venture capital firms are very aware of the marketplace and sensitive to its opportunities. They are, after all, in the business of trying to maximize the return on their investments.

What you will often see is a cluster effect. When biotechnology is hot, firms tend to be more receptive to those proposals. In the past, other hot areas have been stem cell research, e-commerce and nanotechnology.

One key to maximizing the likelihood of obtaining venture capital for your project is to research each VC firm, determine what their current areas of interest are, and then focus on the partner within that firm that may be most receptive to your area of business. Most of the venture capital websites have management team bios on them which will help you make that determination.

Another element in the successful pursuit of venture capital are relationships with the VC firms themselves. If you know one of the partners at the firm, or even know someone who does, then approaching them through this personal contact will provide you with an edge. You would be shocked if you knew how many millions of dollars of venture capital was secured by people during the height of the dot-com craze because they were able to gain access to the VC firms through personal contacts. Make no mistake, ultimately the decision to invest in your company will be made on the merits of its potential, but it never hurts to approach a firm through a friend who has a relationship with them.

If the VC firms pass, then you may wish to pursue angel investors. These are well-financed investors who are willing to finance very early stage opportunities that they believe in. The nice things about angels is they've often started or run very successful businesses in the past, so they have tremendous instincts for what will or will not work.

You can obtain numerous lists of angel investors by conducting an online search using the keywords "list angel investors".

The most important thing you should know about the venture capital acquisition process is that there is an element of subjectivity to it. While many great venture capital firms have tremendous track records, it doesn't mean that your project lacks merit simply because they've passed on it. Often it may just mean that it is not a good fit for them at this time, so don't be discouraged.

Another very important aspect of this process is one that most people applying for capital constantly underestimate. It is crucial that you understand that VC firms place as much stock in your management team's experience and credentials as they do in your idea. In fact, some VCs will place more importance on this, than the idea or business itself. The operating theory is that a great leader or management team can make a success out of a mediocre idea, but a great idea cannot be salvaged by an incompetent team.

If you have a great idea but are somewhat lacking in managerial skills or credentials, then you may wish to attach people to the project that can supplement your own skill set.

Look for people who have a history of starting or running firms that have done well, and ask them to come on board in either an advisory capacity or as a prospective member of your management team. Their inclusion in your business plan will indicate that you are taking the process seriously, and that you are not allowing your ego to prevent you from bringing people on board with expertise which compliments your own.

One thing you can do to increase the likelihood of receiving investment capital is to elevate the media profile of your company or project. Creating media interest in your efforts will help legitimize what you are doing, as well as increase the likelihood that the marketplace will respond favorably to your efforts now that your company has become more recognizable.

When drafting your business plan, there are some things you should do. First, purchase a business plan writing software package. These are tremendously helpful because they will not only guide you through the process, but also contain sample plans.

Another thing to keep in mind when drafting a business plan is not to make your financial forecasts too aggressive. Inexperienced people tend to make wildly exaggerated forecasts and profit predictions in their business plans. They do this in an effort to impress the VCs. Unfortunately, VCs see this all the time, and will interpret it as a "red flag" of inexperience.

CONFIDENTIALITY AGREEMENTS

One of the universal themes which seems to connect the world of organized crime with the world of big business is the tremendous premium that both place on secrecy and discretion.

In the Mafia, members are sworn to secrecy by taking a blood oath designed to assure their allegiance. In some New York and Los Angeles street gangs, members are sworn in by being forced to commit a capital crime.

The reason for all this secrecy is that major organizations understand the economic value of limiting access to important information. The fewer people who know about something, the greater its value.

Confidentiality agreements ensure the preservation of the economic value by limiting access to it. When drafting one, you should have your attorney incorporate clauses which not only preserve the secrecy of your business model and practices in perpetuity, but also prevent the signer from commercially competing with you within a given geographic distance and over a specific period of time (the law differs from state to state, so check with your attorney).

WHAT'S YOURS IS MINE—GANGSTERNOMIC MARKET ACQUISITION

When corporations, monopolies and criminal organizations see a chance for growth, they allow almost nothing to stop them.

Saddam Hussein was so anxious to obtain the oil fields of Kuwait that he invaded the country. His risk/benefit calculation was very straightforward—he always wanted to go after the Saudi oil fields so that he could dominate the world market but knew he couldn't afford that militarily, so he went into Kuwait first. He assumed that once he controlled Kuwait's output, he could use that revenue to build himself up militarily. Once powerful enough, he would roll into Saudi Arabia. His calculation proved erroneous and ultimately cost him everything.

Market share acquisition can be as expensive as it is fraught with peril. When you embark on it you should make the following calculations:

1) Is the cost of growth worth the risk of failure?
2) Is the possibility of failure potentially catastrophic?
3) Is the competitor whose market share I'm going after able to respond in a financially threatening manner?

Criminal Business Model *Gangsters will acquire market share growth with both violence and treachery. That may be effective for them in the short term, but it often generates extraordinary and unforeseeable costs down the road when there is retaliation.*

GangsterNomic Legitimate Business Model Alternative
You can inflict economic shock on your competitors and seize their market share by dramatically altering your product price or features on a random basis.

KNEECAPPING—FIVE GREAT WAYS TO SEIZE A COMPETITOR'S ASSETS

More often than not, sheer competitive effort is no longer enough to overcome the advantage a competitor may possess. This has fueled the growth of "competitor kneecapping".

Competitor kneecapping activity lies in that dark area of commerce somewhere north of business development and just south of anticompetitive behavior. In some ways, it's great because it can level the playing field between a small business and a corporate giant like no other tactic you have ever seen. It is also horrific in its ability to lay waste to a company in ways they cannot always protect themselves against.

Gangsters, dictators and CEOs love it because it is so efficient. People who have been on the receiving end of it despise it. It comes in various forms; here are some examples of competitor kneecapping designed to cripple your enemy:

Raiding Senior Management – Companies try to shield themselves from executive poaching by tying their people up with employee contracts and non-compete clauses. Unfortunately, the one weakness all these contracts have in common is that they eventually expire. As their expiration date approaches, competitors who have been patient often move in with offers that are too attractive to ignore.

Predatory Legislation – Nothing paralyzes a small company with great prospects faster than having a competitor lobby for the introduction of legislation designed to hamstring or thwart their efforts. It happens every year, as large established corporations notice the appearance of a new technology or business model that could blow them out of the water in five years if it is allowed to prosper. They will send a lobbyist to Washington with a suitcase full of cash designed to get a new law introduced. Before you know it, the regulatory climate has changed and is no longer favorable to the new company. Your competition usually ends the process by offering to come in and buy your assets for pennies on the dollar.

Assassination By Rumor – With the advent of the Internet and 500-channel cable TV, it is easier than ever to propagate rumors designed to hurt your competition. The beauty of these tactics is that you never really have to spread libelous or defamatory misinformation. All you need to do is have a well known public relations firm go out and hire a bunch of talking heads, industry analysts and professional media commentators to discuss your new company, product or service in a tone that is skeptical, doubtful and dubious. Gangsters do this all the time by spreading rumors about men in a competitor's gang they claim are working as informants. The beauty of Assassination by Rumor is that it's extremely cancerous. In the criminal world you may know your top lieutenants aren't informants but it's still a very difficult thought to rid yourself of once it's planted. In the corporate world nothing, and I mean nothing scares potential investors away faster than a bad rumor. It's the sort of thing that's killed off more great new companies seeking investment capital than anything else. You're competition usually ends this process by offering to come in and buy your assets for pennies on the dollar

Spurious Patent Infringement Litigation – This is a lawsuit, or often just the threat of a lawsuit, claiming that your technology violates their patent. Ninety-nine percent of the time the claim is completely without merit, and is designed to simply halt your progress and hopefully drive you out of business. Your competition usually offers to end the litigation by acquiring your assets for a fraction of what they are worth.

Controlling Vendor And Subcontractor Output – Sometimes a competitor can choke you off simply by purchasing one hundred percent of the output of one of your critical component subcontractors. Since your company cannot produce its product line without that component, you simply go out of business. Once again, your competition usually ends this process by offering to come in and buy your assets at a substantial discount.

Criminal Business Model In the world of organized crime it is very common for one group to try to seize control of another group's assets with violence, below-market pricing or the execution of some of their competitor's leaders.

GangsterNomic Legitimate Business Model Alternative In the aggressive world of big business it is very common for CEOs to spend as much time plotting the dismemberment of your company as it is for them to try to advance their own products and services. Raiding your management, filing spurious litigation, and assassinating your company's reputation in the media are just a few of the most popular tactics.

ENEMY INSIDE THE GATES

In the seventies and eighties, organized crime figures became so aware of surveillance efforts to record their conversations that they took up a new technique called "hand talking".

Whenever something sensitive needed to be discussed, criminal associates would step outside for a stroll and begin speaking to each other while covering their mouths with their hands. To the casual observer it looked like idiosyncratic behavior. In reality, it was a way of preventing the lip readers brought in by the FBI surveillance teams from reading their lips.

Over the next twenty years, efforts by the FBI to penetrate and record the conversations of criminals included everything from bugging their homes and cars, to placing listening devices on the parking meters and pay phones the gangsters would walk past on their daily strolls.

Penetrating an organization to obtain proprietary information is now seen as standard operating procedure. In the summer of 2005, the highest level Chinese diplomat to defect since 1954 allegedly walked away from the Chinese Consulate in Sydney, Australia, and was reported to have asked for asylum. In a published report, the diplomat was alleged to have claimed that Beijing has approximately 1000 spies living in Australia. If true, then those Chinese spies can be assumed to be gathering industrial secrets designed to strengthen the economic position of China.

It is a hyperaggressive business model which seems to be repeating itself all across the globe. FBI officials have reportedly indicated that they are keeping track of more than 3,000 corporations in the United States that are suspected of gathering information for the Chinese government.

A very important rule of GangsterNomics is that the enemy inside the gate is usually there long before you notice. You cannot have a high-level business conversation with anyone in Silicon Valley these days without the topic of industrial espionage coming up. It's like a torpedo beneath the surface—you know its coming your way, you just can't see it most of the time.

Here are some things you need to know about these types of tactics:

Employee Spy Temps – These are work applicants who try to get hired by your company for the express purpose of stealing industrial secrets. Don't make the mistake of thinking they are always going to be foreign-born nationals. You would be shocked at how easy it is to compromise an existing long-term employee who hasn't received the stock options he thought he was entitled to.

Vendor Spies – They come in all shapes and sizes. It could be the people who repair your vending machines, bring food into your cafeteria or even something much worse. Back in the eighties, some governments would penetrate foreign embassies by sending in copier repair people to place recording devices into the copy machines they were supposed to be fixing. The devices would record copies of every document that was ever placed on the machine. They were so difficult to detect that the only way the embassy could do so was to purchase a copy of the same copier on the open market and then compare their physical weights. When they realized that their copier was 8 ounces heavier, they had it disassembled and did a part by part analysis until they found the device.

Criminal Business Model Stealing information from your competitors in the world of organized crime is now so common, a failure to do so would be viewed as criminal malpractice.

GangsterNomic Legitimate Business Model Alternative Stealing information from your competitors in the corporate world has now become so common that significant efforts to prevent it have to be incorporated into every appropriate business model. Your information technology department may be vigilant, but what protocols does your human resource department have in place to screen for applicants that may have suspicious intentions? What protocols does your communications department have in place to safeguard your phone systems?

CORPORATE ASSASSINS

In the world of organized crime, the most effective assassins are those which can gain the greatest access to the target.

If you have an enemy which absolutely must be destroyed, one of the most cost-effective ways to do it is by cultivating and grooming whistleblowers in their organization.

Whistleblowers are the politically correct corporate assassins of our time. They are the equivalent of a cancer cell with a conscience that suddenly appears on the corporate body and has the ability to silently kill it for all its past misdeeds.

What is interesting about whistleblowers is how cost-effective they are. Corporations will spend millions of dollars annually on research and development as well as marketing and advertising to compete with a corporate adversary. Yet they could accomplish so much more for so much less by simply cultivating and financially backing whistleblowers in their competitor's organization.

What makes whistleblowers so dangerous is that they usually have truth and integrity on their side. What often causes them to fail is the long and expensive whistleblower litigation that forces them to settle rather than continue the protracted court fight—a problem that is often compounded by their inability to find gainful employment during this time.

Financially backing a competitor's whistleblower to the economic finish line of litigation would be one of the greatest investments any company could make. Think about it. You hire a whistleblower that has a court case pending against one of your biggest competitors. By providing them with a steady income, you have made it much easier for them to carry on their legal fight all the way to the trial date.

If they prevail in court, your competitor has taken a major hit which you can financially exploit. If they lose, then you can give them a substantial bonus that quarter; provided they agree to use a portion of it to finance their appeal.

If a corporation wanted to really get GangsterNomically aggressive, it would not only hire as many whistleblowers as possible, but it would pay its law firm to run a full page ad encouraging anyone with a competitor's corporation who has knowledge of wrongdoing that might be addressed with a whistleblower suit, to contact them.

One or two highly placed and well-backed whistleblowers can do more damage to a corporate competitor than hundreds of millions of dollars spent on advertising and new product development. Now that's GangsterNomics.

HAVE YOU EVER BEEN CONVICTED OF A FELONY?

There is a growing trend that both the world of organized crime and the legitimate corporate world seem to share, and that is the deliberate hiring of felons. I see growing evidence of this in several industries.

One of the most clever new television shows in development is called **Danger Island** (see **www.DangerIsland.TV**). It is a next-generation reality television show in which twelve real-life former felons are placed on an island where they will compete for a million dollar prize to be given to the victim of the winner's last crime. I mention it because the legal, logistical and security considerations involved in working with felons are not trivial.

Here are some examples of situations in which felons were knowingly hired for legitimate reasons:

Computer Hackers – Countless Fortune 500 companies have hired former hackers to help them fortify their computing systems and fight off the intrusive efforts of other hackers.

Motion Picture and Television Consultants – This has been a growing trend for quite some time in both gangster genre movies and television shows. Studios will bring in real mobsters and convicted criminals, and use them as consultants to help elevate the level of realism in certain scenes and scripts.

Security – Often times when operating in a foreign country, corporations will be forced to deal with countless criminal threats. Some companies will hire one group of criminals to defend them from another. This often happens in third world countries which are overrun with paramilitary groups or kidnapping syndicates.

Convicted CEOs, Actors And Politicians – There is a growing tendency in the marketplace to hire prominent individuals who have been convicted of felonies and have completed serving their sentences. Actors who've done prison time are often viewed by the studios as having an enhanced market value because their fans are even more curious to see them in the movies again. In a strange display of irony, politicians who have served jail time and then run for office again are viewed by some members of the community as having an enhanced level of street credibility, which they feel makes them worthy of consideration for office. Prominent businesspeople who've made mountains of money for a company before they did their jail time are often viewed as individuals whose overall performance record far outweighs the isolated incident that put them in jail. Boards of directors are so tempted by their money-making skills, they are willing to overlook a felony conviction in a high level executive that they'd never overlook in a janitorial job applicant.

In another display of tremendous irony, while corporations are now increasing their hiring of convicted felons, criminal organizations are now hiring more legitimate businesspeople than ever before. Some of them don't even know they are working for a criminal enterprise, while others are brought in fully aware that they've been hired to put a legitimate face on a very dubious enterprise.

It is a classic convergence of two worlds which seem to be growing less dissimilar with each passing day.

DOING BUSINESS WITH THE DARK SIDE

History is full of examples where legitimate companies or governments decided to do business with the dark side of organized crime. Lucky Luciano was approached by the U.S. government during World War II to discuss his ability to help America obtain military intelligence on German troop movements in Italy prior to our invasion. He reportedly did provide the information, and was eventually rewarded by Thomas Dewey with easy time in prison and a commutation of his sentence that resulted in his being able to leave the United States so he could live in Italy.

In corporate America, not a day goes by when some CEO or owner isn't confronted with the possibility of doing business with organized crime. Sometimes it's out of economic necessity when they borrow money no one else will loan them; sometimes they will request help in muscling a union boss into succumbing to terms that are more favorable than would ordinarily be possible. Under darker circumstances, organized crime connections will even be used to assassinate a competitor or smuggle slave laborers into the United States to help get a new business off the ground.

The end result of these unholy partnerships is often both a loss of control and a perpetual indebtedness to the gangsters which provided the help.

In some post cold war nations, the governments themselves are now controlled by organized crime figures who have risen up through the economic ranks. Conducting business with these governments is a bit like openly dealing with criminals on a sunny day. They will attempt to project a strange and false sense of legitimacy, but deep down inside no one is being fooled.

JURISDICTION SHOPPING

When criminal organizations embark on what's known as a "long con", they will search for a jurisdiction in which the sentencing guidelines for a conviction are minimal. Long cons tend to take time to execute, and being in one location for a considerable length of time increases one's likelihood of arrest.

Jurisdiction shopping allows one to compare the sentencing guidelines for various countries and regions. There are some nations which will sentence you to life for a crime that will get you a slap on the wrist in another country.

On a corporate level, jurisdiction shopping involves other criteria. When selecting a country or city to conduct business, corporations will often calculate the civil and criminal penalties for the following:

Dumping Toxic Waste – There are some countries in which the authorities are paid to completely ignore this sort of activity. Manufacturing plants located near rivers in such countries have been known to cause them to turn from a liquid water color to a brownish semi-solid gelatin.

Exploiting Child Labor – Some areas of the world will allow corporations to hire and work underage children in conditions that can only be described as medieval.

Tax Abatement – While shopping for the most aggressive tax abatement incentive used to be considered standard operating procedure when looking for a new location, now it has taken on a different meaning. In some circumstances, tax abatement has become the new code phrase for "we wish to pay no taxes at all, and we'd like the local government to absorb a portion of our construction costs in return for our creating jobs".

CONDUCTING GANGSTERNOMIC
BUSINESS OFFSHORE

Doing business overseas is often easier than in the United States.

Mind you, this doesn't apply to all countries, but in many places the reduced barriers to entry created by NAFTA and the advantages posed by exchange rates are so favorable, it is difficult to ignore.

Filming a movie in a country like New Zealand is much less expensive than filming in the U.S. It has been widely reported that Quentin Tarantino shot a significant portion of "Kill Bill Vol. 1" on a Beijing sound stage. As a result, his production expenses were reportedly reduced by 85%, compared to what it would have cost to film in Los Angeles.

There seems to be a prevailing sentiment that conducting business offshore is something that is usually done by big business. While the majority of the big deals you read about in the press are initiated by major conglomerates, in reality, there are countless small and independent American companies doing business overseas.

Most people think this is a result of the Internet, but that's just part of the equation. In reality, the phenomenon has been fueled by the advent of email, inexpensive overseas labor costs, NAFTA and some highly advantageous exchange rates.

Countries with favorable exchange rates or low labor costs are:

Australia
Brazil
Canada
China
Czech Republic
Hungary
Mexico
Romania
Ukraine

The thing to remember when conducting business overseas is that foreigners have a very keen eye for weakness and incompetence, and will exploit it very quickly. If you are going to do business overseas, always remember to practice many of the applicable rules outlined in this book.

DOING BUSINESS WITH THE RUSSIAN KGB

Doing business in Russia is like doing business during wartime. Anything can happen, and probably will. This poses both an extraordinary risk and the potential for incredible rewards.

The reason so many gangsters leave Russia, come to the United States and become millionaires within a year is that by comparison, doing business here seems so much easier for them. The same thing can be said for a lot of businessmen who come here from the Middle East.

What they both have in common is that whether you're in Russia or the Middle East, you are literally taking your life in your hands each day you go out and conduct business. This has a way of not only hardening you, but also dramatically increasing your ability to endure risk.

Once you have been shot few times, dealing with taxes, high interest rates, difficult customers and vendors seems like a walk in the park. In parts of the U.S. Midwest, for example, Middle Easterners open up liquor stores and gas stations in neighborhoods that are so tough that even the police dogs wear bullet proof vests. Within twelve months these businesses will not only be thriving but are generating enough revenue to open up another business just down the street.

In Moscow, things are so difficult that even real estate agents need bodyguards. Whether you are representing yourself as an independent businessman or representing a major multinational corporation, the challenges can be unlike anything you have ever anticipated.

Here are just a few of the issues you need to keep in mind when working in Russia:

Establishing A Presence – You can use your own staff to do this, but statistically speaking you will have a greater chance for success if you embark on a joint venture with a Russian company. They will not only have a better command of the laws and customs, but they will also be on a first name basis with the people who run the local bureaucracies.

KGB – Go to Lubyanka Square in downtown Moscow and you will find the headquarters building of the former KGB. For many decades, it was the home of one of the toughest and most cunning intelligence agencies in the world. After the cold war ended, many members of the KGB took their political contacts, clout and resources, and went into business for themselves. Today they have risen to the very top of the 'new Russia' and in many instances, are the "go to" people for getting things done. If you are doing anything worth noticing on a business level in Russia, they'll probably know all about you shortly after you get off the plane. These people work in almost every aspect of

Russian industry, and are so well-connected that they can be a tremendous asset.

DOING BUSINESS IN MIDDLE EASTERN WAR ZONES

If you are going to pursue serious profits, you must assume serious risk. The Middle East can provide you with ample quantities of each.

First, I will state the obvious and recommend that you refrain from conducting business in any of the ongoing war zones. The problem isn't just the risk to personal safety—conducting business in an active war zone without military protection will mean that every warlord within a hundred miles will steal from you. After they have stolen everything you have, they will kidnap you and demand a ransom from your family or employer. When the representative from your employer or insurance company shows up with the ransom money, they'll take that and then kidnap him. There is no end to it.

At this moment, there are some countries in the Middle East which still present a reasonable level of potential risk and reward. They are:

Kuwait
Qatar
Jordan
Saudi Arabia

If you are thinking about conducting business in any of these areas, you should always consider partnering with an American company that has already established a presence there. Alternatively, you may consider partnering with a company in the host country.

Before you proceed, make certain to consult with your attorney, the U.S. State Department, as well as the embassy of the country that you are interested in doing business with.

As you read this, the situation over there is rapidly changing so make certain to weight all the risk factors very carefully with the experts you speak with.

THE PROHIBITIVE COST OF ETHICAL BUSINESS

There are some areas of the globe in which the cost of conducting business ethically is almost prohibitive. Some of these GangsterNomic ethical hot zones have already received a great deal of press. Places like the former Soviet Union, Eastern Europe, the Middle East, and of course, much of Central and South America.

In many of these zones, trying to conduct business ethically has been complicated tremendously by two factors. The first is that law enforcement has often become indistinguishable from organized crime. The second, and equally problematic one, is that the level of corruption has become so pervasive that by the time you factor in the cost of all the bribes and payoffs, you can easily double or triple your conventional costs of doing business. Add to that the fact that many of these payoffs must continue for months or even years, and it quickly becomes apparent that the costs are just prohibitive.

What many multinationals are now doing when they go into a foreign country is to secure the services of intermediaries. These "consultants" will provide two services. The first is that they possess an expertise in knowing whose financial "needs" must be "addressed", and how much it will cost to "address" them before you can do business in their country. The second is that these "consultants" will provide a layer of insulation between all the parties involved, in case there is excessive press scrutiny or some other complication.

PSEUDO-SLAVE LABOR

One business model that seems to have become very popular in the worlds of organized crime and corporations is the practice of restructuring. Once one of the most benign and innocuous words in business, restructuring has become a code word for something far more sinister.

In the criminal world, it used to mean killing the folks at the top of the organization and replacing them with the people who've killed them. In the corporate world, it used to mean modifying the organizational chart or changing the way business was done so as to squeeze out a few more percentage points of profit at the end of the year.

All of that has changed. An unholy economic convergence between organized crime and the corporate sector has resulted from them both becoming obsessed with exploiting what can only be described as "pseudo-slave labor".

In organized crime, an organization will smuggle in hundreds of illegals who will be forced to work in a factory to pay off the indebtedness they incurred by being brought to the U.S. This low wage servitude can go on for more than a decade in some cases. Workers who wish to leave or quit are often threatened with violence.

Many corporations will adopt the mirror image of this business model. They will bring a new plant to some remote region of the earth that barely qualifies as a third world country. They'll then supply jobs that elevate the workers a notch or two above destitution, but prevent them from ever really advancing themselves economically. In many cases, they will be forced to endure work hours and conditions that would never be tolerated in civilized countries.

On the surface, the employers will claim their employees are free to make their own choices, and are earning a wage that is superior to that which they would have made previously. In reality, their wages are deliberately kept at a point which can best be described as the "hovering poverty level". That is a wage level designed to keep you alive but prevent you from accumulating enough wealth or assets to ever really leave. It is this wage level that systematically maintains the "pseudo-slave labor" status of every worker there.

What's interesting is that in many of these scenarios, the wages are so incredibly low that you could double them without significantly impacting the bottom line of the company. Employers will refrain from doing this because it would create a genuinely mobile and prosperous middle class in those communities and that would diminish the company's ability to control them as employees.

The employees may not be shackled by chains like real slaves, but their wages and employment conditions maintain a virtual stranglehold on them just as effectively.

What is so very shortsighted about this business model is that it often fails to create a market for the very products it manufactures. The more American jobs are moved overseas, the less people there are in the U.S. that are able to purchase the goods manufactured by "pseudo-slave labor". It is an accelerating downward spiral that very few people seem to be addressing on a policy level.

When practiced by criminals and corporations alike, the act of building these "pseudo-slave labor" centers seems to create communities that are cloaked in a false veneer of opportunity, when in reality they are providing the exact opposite. It's as gangster as gangster gets, and is one of the best examples of contemporary GangsterNomics you will ever see.

ELIMINATING AMERICA AS THE MIDDLEMAN

A group of foreign businessmen recently arrived in the United States and decided to take an unscheduled tour of one of our national retail chains. As they were walking down the aisles checking out the prices of various items, they grew increasingly disturbed by what they saw. Things that they were manufacturing in China for fifty cents were being sold in this store for twenty dollars. This growing revelation has resulted in a paradigm shift amongst Asian corporations and government officials.

As their manufacturing power and cash reserves have increased in recent years, many Asian companies have decided to eliminate the American middleman entirely by trying to purchase U.S. companies.

Recent attempts to acquire American computer manufacturers, oil companies and national retailers have emboldened foreign companies to believe they no longer need to limit themselves to the manufacturing of goods for the U.S. market. They can dramatically increase their revenues by acquiring U.S. companies which sell directly to American consumers.

Now instead of making fifty cents on that item, they can collect the full twenty dollars. This is an extraordinary GangsterNomic escalation in the dismantling of the U.S. economy because it causes erosion at both ends.

On one side you are eroding the domestic job base by shipping them overseas where wages are 90% lower. At the other end of the economic engine you are eliminating American ownership of companies that generate domestic revenue and taxes by selling them to foreign companies who are already supplying the cheap labor.

Absent the immediate passage of legislation designed to limit activity like this, it is clear that it will continue to gain momentum until it threatens the future economic sovereignty of the United States. On the GangsterNomic scale of those activities which generate long-term economic damage, this one ranks near the top.

BANKRUPTCY FOR PROFIT

A very fast growing new GangsterNomic phenomenon is known as bankruptcy for profit. It is perfectly legal and seems to be giving birth to an entirely new growth industry.

Here's how it works. A corporation will bring a new CEO on board to help guide the company over the coming years. Shortly after the new CEO takes over, the company's performance begins to decline.

Within twenty-four months the decline is so severe that the company is teetering on bankruptcy. Declaring that all other options have been exhausted, the CEO initiates bankruptcy proceedings in what he will publicly declare to be a last ditch effort to salvage those portions of the company that can be saved.

As the company goes through bankruptcy, offers are made by third parties to acquire portions of it for pennies on the dollar. While these buyers are publicly described as "white knights", in reality there is something far less coincidental going on.

If you perform an exhaustive background check, you will find that the CEO hired by the company had often presided over several other major corporations that performed terribly and may have even gone into bankruptcy. The truth of the matter is that it is his specialty. He is deliberately hired for his ability to diminish a company's performance and drive down its market value so other insiders can move in and acquire the assets inexpensively. Once acquired, those assets are then properly managed back to financial health so their new owners can reap the rewards.

The entire operation is set up to disgorge highly valuable corporate assets from a deliberately crippled company so that their new owners can exploit them. If you go back through the headlines, you'll see example after example of once great companies which seems to implode overnight only to emerge from bankruptcy smaller and leaner. Do a detailed analysis of who owns some of the assets that were sold off during or after the bankruptcy, and many of the names will prove very interesting.

ARTIFICIALLY INSEMINATED CORRUPTION

In the world of organized crime it is often easier to access and seize a new market if one can first gain control of it. Traditionally, legitimate corporations entering a new market would do so with a great deal of preparation, strategy and hard work. Criminals rarely have that kind of patience. Their approach is a bit more accelerated.

Because criminals are often competing with other criminals for the same opportunity, it is imperative that they move as quickly as possible. That means seizing control. Under normal circumstances, any attempt to do that would be met with a quick phone call to law enforcement, but that would only complicate matters.

Instead, what they will do is artificially inseminate corruption into the situation. First they will identify the authority figures and major decision makers. Then they will shorten that list of names down to the people who appear to have an exploitable weakness. For some it's gambling, women, or just plain greed.

The individual will then be lured into a circumstance designed to compromise them with an enormous gambling debt, pregnancy, or criminal act that leaves them exposed to subsequent threats of blackmail. Once they are vulnerable on that level, it is usually much easier to secure their participation.

Gaining control of an entire corporation is relatively easy once you have compromised the key players, which often means getting to the CEO or CFO.

Back in the sixties, organized crime allegedly gained control of an entire labor union by compromising its founding leader. Then it gained control of their pension fund and used it to underwrite whatever projects they embarked on. Compromising a single individual provided them with access to hundreds of millions of dollars of pension money.

Controlling entire industries is only slightly more difficult. Instead of identifying key corporate players, you target key industry choke points. For some it may mean distribution; for other industries it may mean financing. Once you establish those choke points you compromise them, and that gives you control of everything.

That's how organized crime does it. In the world of GangsterNomics it is accomplished in a completely legal fashion by using vast sums of money to purchase people's loyalty. If that doesn't work, than you corrupt them with a quantity of money that exceeds their ability to say no. Once you have acquired their loyalty, the momentum tends to build fairly quickly in your favor until you finally seize control.

CORPORATE MISBEHAVIOR OVERSEAS

Most people assume that the principal reason corporations do business overseas is the lure of low labor costs. That is just part of it. The ugly truth is, companies and criminal organizations love setting up overseas because it's possible to get away with so much more there.

If you are involved in bootlegging or producing knockoffs, chances are you're operating out of Eastern Europe or

Asia. If it's drugs, then chances are you are shuttling back and forth between the Caribbean and Central America. If you're involved in the illegal sale of arms and munitions, then you're probably in the Middle East. Stolen information your game? Odds are you're in the Ukraine or Russia.

Shady corporate entities will set up operations overseas in areas that allow them to work relatively unimpeded by the efforts of law enforcement and regulatory agencies. In fact, if a regulatory agency were to fax one of these companies a complaint letter alleging some sort of misconduct and threatening a fine, the recipients might very well hurt themselves from all the laughter.

Some countries have entire regions which are governed by warlords or corrupt officials whose full-time job it is to protect the illegal operations running in that area. Keeping them safe ensures the uninterrupted flow of money that is kicked back to them.

Another benefit of operating in these overseas gray zones is the freedom they offer from litigation. If the bribes these companies pay to the government officials aren't enough to keep the lawyers at bay, then many of them are set up to disappear on a moment's notice should that become necessary.

SIZE DOES MATTER

The trajectory of GangsterNomic activity is both upward and accelerated. Not only is the size and frequency of ruthless criminal and corporate behavior increasing, but it is displaying an ability to evolve so rapidly that it's difficult to monitor.

Just when you think the nature of things can't possibly get any worse, the situation devolves into something which proves you wrong.

Case in point: in mid-2004, a group of very sophisticated hackers hammered away at the computer system of a major Japanese bank located in England. The plan was to allegedly steal more than $400 million dollars and then wire the money to ten different accounts they had set up around the globe. The BBC News reported that the plan almost worked until it was discovered by cyber police working for the British National Hi Tech Crime Unit.

The criminals were allegedly using keylogger spyware that was stealing password information from bank computers.

What's interesting about this attempt is that, had it succeeded, it would have been ten times larger than the record-holding $50 million dollar theft from Belfast's Northern Bank.

As the intensity of GangsterNomic activity increases it is clear that both the legal and illegal efforts being embarked on all across the globe are becoming more ambitious and aggressive in scope.

INVISIBLE CORPORATIONS

The latest trend in the world of organized crime is the establishment of invisible corporations. They have tremendous advantages which allow gangsters to conduct business in ways which may totally confound the efforts of law enforcement, as well as legitimate corporations trying to compete with them in the marketplace.

Invisible corporations are temporary entities set up to conduct business in a highly mobile, clandestine and untraceable fashion. Here's how they work:

No Incorporation – This entity is almost never incorporated. If it is, then the corporation is set up with shell companies based out of the Caribbean or the Middle East. An investigation into the names listed on the corporation papers usually reveals them to be deceased or non-existent.

Payments – Payments are usually transacted through a commercial payment service. If checks are used or collected, they are usually cleared through banks in the Middle East which will launder the money and forward it to accounts set up in New York.

Communications – Landlines are never used. Standard operating procedure is to use a combination of three items: 1) a disposable cell phone, 2) a pager, and 3) a calling card purchased with a fake name. These three items are usually replaced every seven to ten days to impede the efforts of anyone trying to locate the owners.

Multiple Fake ID's – Most of the people involved in this sort of business have provided themselves with an extra layer of protection by setting up multiple identities for themselves. This allows them to slip away quickly under another name, should their previous identity become compromised.

Aggressive Kickbacks – Invisible corporations will also kick money back in very significant sums to the government officials providing them with protection. What they're often paying for is the right to receive a warning call in the middle of the night telling them trouble is on the way. It's the sort of advance notice that can provide them with the precious hour needed for escape.

What is interesting about the invisible corporations used by gangsters is how they are being mirrored by the legitimate corporate world in its establishment of virtual corporations.

VIRTUAL CORPORATIONS

Virtual corporations are the legitimate counterpart of invisible corporations. They are typically incorporated in

Delaware. Most of them maintain their presence online with a website, rather than set up a physical address in a brick and mortar building. The principals and employees are usually scattered all across the country and linked by cell phone and email.

Many virtual corporations are set up to exist only for the duration of a specific project. For example, rock bands or movie production companies will set them up to operate during the life of the tour or movie production, and then the team will dissolve upon its completion.

Setting up a virtual corporation will result in a sizable savings over the establishment of a conventional one. Eliminating the need for a building, landlines and utilities will lower overhead and allow them to become more responsive to a fast-changing marketplace.

Criminal Business Model *The establishment of Invisible Corporations allows criminal entities to operate in a clandestine fashion and evade the efforts of law enforcement trying to stop them.*

GangsterNomic Legitimate Business Model Alternative *Legitimate business entities are setting up Virtual Corporations for several reasons. The first is that it allows them to avoid the cost of acquiring a physical address as well as paying for utilities and landlines. It also allows their staff to be highly mobile and dispersed throughout a wide geographic area.*

NOMADIC CORPORATIONS

Nomadic corporations will conceal their existence the way invisible corporations do, but they will also keep their personnel, assets and money in a perpetual state of motion designed to make them very difficult to locate, identify or apprehend.

Their funds will be kept in a staggered state of perpetual motion by moving them from one banking center to another over brief intervals. They will perform what's known as "account hopping" between banks in Switzerland, Liechtenstein, Cayman Island, Panama, Gibraltar, Isle of Man, Israel and Asia. The accounts will also be established in new names, so as to sever the link to the previous name of record and to make tracking more difficult. Numbered accounts will also be used to further conceal the money trail and make pursuit futile. The account hopping occurs over brief and irregular time periods, so there is no discernable pattern or cycle that would assist investigators in any way.

Assets are, whenever possible, converted into cash or securities which can then be moved electronically from jurisdiction to jurisdiction. Years ago in the movies, you would always see criminals stealing bearer bonds because of their unregistered and anonymous ownership. They were often depicted as a convenient way to anonymously transport a great deal of money. Today, bearer bonds are being phased out of existence and replaced by registered bonds.

With regards to the personnel involved in nomadic corporations, they tend to move electronically far more often than they do geographically. They will accomplish this by routinely changing their identities, ISPs, email addresses, cell phones, phone numbers, pager numbers and mail drop locations. While they can physically remain within the same city for months, they can alter their virtual or electronic location as often as they like, depending on how paranoid they are. Using a Voice Over Internet Protocol phone, it is very easy to alter their phone number and area code to make it appear as though they are located in a different city. Nomadics can purchase dozens of phone numbers with area codes that appear to originate in cities all over the world, yet all link back to wherever they are.

The key to this business model is the rapidity of movement and the frequency of change. That's what makes this type of activity possible.

If you think this sort of behavior is limited to the criminal world, then think again. The Bahamas, Cayman Islands, Switzerland and other banking centers contain dozens of boutique law firms whose specialty is the creation, administration, and liquidation of anonymously controlled corporations set up by overseas entities that wish to preserve their anonymity and dubious tax status.

Criminal Business Model *The establishment of Nomadic Corporations allows criminal entities to use speed and perpetual relocation to evade the efforts of law enforcement trying to locate and stop them.*

GangsterNomic Legitimate Business Model Alternative *Legitimate corporations tend to employ perpetual motion on a different level. Rather than use it to evade detection, they tend to employ it to move capital from one financial market to another in a constant search for the highest rate of return on their capital. Individuals tend to use this form of movement to protect their assets from those who have court judgements or unfavorable divorce decrees pending against them in other jurisdictions.*

THE CANADIAN LOTTERY SCAM / BUSINESS MODEL

The rate and sophistication with which organized crime is adopting modern business models and employing them to scam unsuspecting victims is unprecedented.

One of the newest and fastest-growing cons is called "The Canadian Lottery" scam. It is usually originated out of Toronto or Montreal because of their relatively lax telemarketing fraud sentencing guidelines.

Here's how it works: a telemarketing fraud team will purchase a new "mooch list". This is a readily available list containing the names and phone numbers of people who routinely fill out sweepstakes coupons and contest entry forms. They will call these people (many of which tend to be senior citizens and housewives), and tell them they've won the Canadian Lottery. They will tell them that the Canadian government has a program which pays most of the taxes when a senior citizen wins the lottery, but that they will still have to pay $10,000 of it.

The overjoyed senior citizen is then told to send the money via wire transfer. When they do, they will receive a phone call a few days later providing them with some more good news. They're told that the first place winner has been disqualified, and that if they send in another $75,000 they will receive the $2,000,000 first prize.

All of this business is transacted via cell phones, pagers and wire transfer agents. While it's often the highly convincing and trustworthy voice of someone pretending to be a Canadian Lottery official at the other end of the phone line that begins this process, it is really the sophistication of the business model and technology that allows them to get away with this kind of theft.

The FBI has recently estimated that more than a hundred million dollars has been stolen using this model, and more than forty percent of the funds being wired to the Toronto area are from people all over the United States who have been taken in by this Lottery Scam.

MONSTER GANGSTER VERSUS MONSTER GANGSTER

A number of years ago, the father of a future U.S. President was reported to have walked into Chicago's East Ambassador Hotel wearing a disguise and seeking a favor. Press accounts indicate that he was at the hotel to meet with Sam Giancana. He found out that another mobster had allegedly put a hit out on him, because he claimed the father had backed out of some deals he made. In an effort to win over Sam's assistance in getting the hit removed, the father allegedly told him that when his son became President of the United States, he would be very indebted to Sam for saving his father's life. Within days, Sam was reported to have called the other mobster and told him how much more influence their organization would have if they had a strong connection in the White House. The hit was removed that week.

Regardless of where you are in your career arc, there will come a time when you have to compete with someone who is so ruthless, hard core and well-connected that you have to resort to extreme measures to defeat them.

When these situations occur, they often require super-aggressive tactics designed to rise to the occasion. In the world of organized crime, it usually means resorting to violence. Since that is not an option in the legitimate world of business, you have to resort to something even more powerful. Innovation.

Below is a list of GangsterNomic tactics and business models—think of them as thermonuclear weapons. They are extremely powerful, and once they are detonated there's no going back.

Release Publicly Available Political Information – When there are very serious dollars at stake between you and your corporate adversaries, it's often common to see one or even both sides invoke the assistance of politicians. What usually happens is that the politicians will then initiate public hearings, or they will introduce legislation designed to compromise you. When that happens, one of the things you should consider doing is ascertaining how much money, if any, your competitor has donated to the politician working on his behalf, and then release that information. The information is usually already public. When you have shed renewed light on it, it will cause the politician working against you to lose credibility. Instead of just being a public servant, he is now viewed as a paid representative of your competitor. Obtain the pre-approval of your attorney before considering this course of action.

Personalize The War – If your adversary has skeletons in his or her closet that might facilitate your efforts, you should hire a private detective to uncover them—just be fully prepared for them to reciprocate with similar tactics. Everyone will condemn this tactic, but there has not been a major political campaign or corporate takeover in the last century in which it hasn't been explored. Needless to say, obtain the pre-approval of your attorney before considering this course of action.

Embark On A High Profile Negative Ad Campaign – This is an open declaration of war. It will also bring a halt to whatever settlement negotiations you may be involved in. Ironically, it can also escalate things to such a level that it brings both parties back to the negotiation table and cause the re-initiation of settlement talks. Obtain the pre-approval of your attorney before considering this course of action

The problem with going toe-to-toe with a corporate gangster as resolute as yourself, is that it can lead to the kind of escalation of ill will that can easily spiral out of the control of both parties.

It can also ignite such hostility that people start behaving in an economically irrational manner. If enough damage is done, they may completely lose sight of the financial goals and spend more money trying to destroy you than they will ever make by beating you in the marketplace.

Ego and pride at this level can inflate to such biblical proportions that they start making multimillion-dollar decisions based on how good destroying you will make them feel. They would never admit it, but believe me, it happens.

This sort of behavior is almost epidemic in large family businesses where siblings or opposing generations will fight for control of the organization. What ends up often happening is that their business decision-making process becomes driven by the deep-rooted emotions stemming from their childhood.

THE ART OF CHARACTER DREDGING

When a conflict between two entities escalates, the attacks will eventually become personal. You see it in corporate America just as often as you do in the worlds of organized crime and politics.

It's called "character dredging", and it is a process designed to dig through every aspect of a competitor's life until something so illicit and compromising is found, the mere threat of disclosure is enough to undermine their ability to compete with you. This tactic has kept countless people who would have made very strong political candidates from even considering a run for office.

It usually begins with the hiring of one or more private detectives whose full-time responsibility it will be to investigate everything about you—everyone who has ever known you and everyone you've ever done business with. Here's the short list of their directives:

People You've Slept With – They will talk to anyone and everyone you may have slept with in an effort to find something unconventional about your sex life. Ideally, they will be able to dig up nude photos of you, which can be leaked out over the Internet. They'll also investigate the other people your former sexual partners have slept with in an effort to indirectly tie you to some implied inappropriateness.

People You've Done Inappropriate Business With – Efforts will be made to both uncover any fraudulent business activity you've ever been involved in as well as try to intimidate anyone you are currently doing business with. The idea is to plant seeds of doubt in their minds, and cause them to take their business elsewhere.

Embarrassing Medical Records – The search will focus on obtaining information about your medical and psychological history that can be used to humiliate you by leaking it to the press.

Legal Records / Divorce Records – These speak for themselves. Sometimes they are sealed, but often times they aren't. If you have been involved in a contentious divorce or legal battle with someone in the past, than this is also information they will attempt to use.

What's ironic about character dredging is that Americans have become so desensitized to the constant media onslaught of one scandal after another, the ability to destroy someone with this tactic has been greatly diminished over the last few years.

A perfect example of this diminished ability is the way that character dredging was used in an attempt to destroy President Clinton, and completely failed to do so. His opponents flooded the airwaves and the judicial system with one allegation after another, and they were all eventually neutralized, ignored, or proven inconsequential.

GANGSTERNOMIC WEAPONS ARSENAL

Today's weapons arsenal for major corporations and criminal enterprises tend to contain many of the same tools. Some of them are borne of a need for self-preservation, while others serve different purposes. As you might expect, some of the weapons are offensive, some defensive, and the rest...well, those are the most interesting of all.

General Counsel – Your choice of general counsel will often be the determining factor in your ability to prevail in a legal conflict. Counsels with considerable experience as litigators tend to do better than those whose primary emphasis is negotiation and settlement. The litigators tend to be more aggressive and successful in extracting more favorable terms when a case is finally settled or won.

Lobbyists – Having a very well-connected lobbyist on retainer is extremely important if the nature of your problem can be addressed with legislation. Fortunately, there are very few significant financial issues that cannot be resolved favorably with legislation if enough money is spent.

Intelligence – Some organizations retain an outside agency, while others develop an internal department to gather intelligence. Most operate under a directive designed to gather as much information about their competitor and the economic landscape as possible. Sometimes the information they gather may be as simple as knowing the precise launch date of a competitor's new product. It doesn't sound significant, but even something like that is enough to arm you with tremendous decision-making options. Other times it will be something more significant, like learning that one of your competitor's key employees is thinking of leaving.

Cash – Perhaps the greatest weapon of all—its ability to solve technical, legal and political problems borders on the magical. When all other options have failed, never underestimate the ability of cash to get you to the finish line.

Criminal Business Model *The arsenal of criminal organizations tends to contain both weapons and violence.*

GangsterNomic Legitimate Business Model Alternative
The corporate weapons arsenal usually contains political contacts, lobbyists, cash, and sophisticated intelligence gathering capability.

THE MOTHER OF ALL GANGSTERNOMIC TACTICS

Finance your own political candidate. This is the ultimate power play. If all else fails, then the final move on the chess board means financing a political candidate who is completely aligned with your agenda, and will back it very aggressively.

Here are some estimated campaign costs:

Small To Medium Sized Mayoral Campaign - $500,000
Large City Mayoral Campaign - $2,000,000
Small To Medium Sized State Gubernatorial
Campaign - $5,000,000
Large State Gubernatorial Campaign - $10,000,000
U.S. Senate Campaign - $50,000,000
U.S. Presidential Campaign - $250,000,000 +

Here is the risk-reward calculation that usually precedes an undertaking of this magnitude:

What will the economic impact on my bottom line be if my candidate fails to win? What usually happens is that your political and corporate adversaries will escalate their efforts to undermine you. The rewards one reaps from having one's own candidate in office are virtually incalculable. Beyond all the obvious benefits, the one that is most fulfilling tends to be watching your enemies cower in the shadow of your newfound power.

TOPLESS INVESTORS

Every day of the week, individuals and financial organizations scour the earth looking for someone to invest in their latest opportunity. They will buy postal mailing lists, phone lists and email lists. You name it and they'll buy it, if they think there's even a small chance that people on the list will have the money it takes to invest.

The number of people in North America looking for investment funding is staggering. Everyone from major Wall Street Investment banks to street level investors are chasing the same dead-end leads. Stock traders, mortgage companies, salesmen, real estate companies and private investment clubs are just a few of them—not a single creative one in the bunch. They all buy the same lists of dentists, doctors, retirees, high-income zip code homeowners, etc. These are people who have put Call Blocker on their phones, and routinely throw a dozen mail solicitations in the garbage each day.

One group of people I have never seen aggressively approached is topless dancers. Think about it for a minute. An unattractive stripper can still make $500 per night. If she's stunning, she can make $5000 per night. Think that is an exaggeration? Go to Las Vegas and watch the money flow in some of the topless bars. It's as though someone came in and sprinkled "You Will Lose Your Mind" dust into the eyes of the men who go there.

A single three-minute lap dance is now as much as $60 dollars in some Silicon Valley strip clubs. Do the math. It's all in cash, and for the most part it has got only three places to go: drugs, alcohol, or bail money for their crazy boyfriends.

If you have a genuine and legitimate investment opportunity that you would like to bring to the attention of a group of prospective investors, these are the folks you should consider.

Just don't make the mistake of being condescending or rude. While these women may not have MBAs, many of them are very good with money. The smart ones purchase expensive homes and own safety deposit boxes full of stacked hundred dollars bills.

SOLICITING A STRIPPER

If you are going to attempt to solicit topless dancers with a new investment opportunity, then here is what I suggest.

Most of these women work five to six nights a week and tend to sleep until three p.m. Rent out a dinner hall at an upscale hotel and invite them to a free luncheon seminar. Tell them they can bring a friend.

Whatever you do, do not serve alcohol. The last thing on earth you want to do is serve alcohol to a dancer. It's like pouring gasoline on an open fire. Hire someone fairly prominent to attend the presentation and sit on the stage with you. If they introduce you, that's even better. It can be a local celebrity, sports figure or a well-known businessperson.

Make your presentation and then do a Q & A. The thing about topless dancers is that they tend to talk a lot. This is great because if you can get a dozen of them to invest and things go well, you will have hundreds of them calling you in no time at all.

A word of caution: dancers always have their radar on, and can smell nonsense a mile away. When you make your presentation, you are going to be facing a room full of some of the most beautiful women you've ever seen. Do not flirt with any of them. If they so much as suspect that you're interested in them romantically, you will never see a dime of investment money; quite the contrary—they will go out with you, move in with you, get added to your credit cards and before you know it, they've got a ton of your hundred dollar bills stashed away in their safety deposit box.

DEGENERATE GAMBLERS AS INVESTORS

When it comes to potential investors, there is one group that stands out so prominently that it's almost without equal.

This group of people not only have the cash, but they also have a very high tolerance for risk. Most importantly, they are almost never approached or solicited by the army of people and companies out their looking for investment funding. The are degenerate gamblers.

As a group of prospective investors, these people are a gift from God. They love to gamble. They are addicted to risk. Their eyes glaze over when they're tantalized by the prospect of winning big. Best of all, most people out there don't realize how easy this group is to access and solicit for an investment.

You can do what some folks do, which is hire someone to drive through and record the license plate numbers of vehicles parked in casino lots. They then cross-reference that information to obtain the names, phone numbers and mailing addresses of the vehicle owners.

Another method is to get their information by having beautiful women approach the people exiting the high-roller gaming rooms of the casinos, and offering them a free dinner for two to a special investment seminar.

The last and most effective way to compile a list of gamblers is to purchase a list of people who subscribe to gambling publications. Cross-reference them with the names of homeowners, and you will have a gold mine of a list to work with.

The great thing about gamblers is that if they see something which truly appeals to them, they will take money out of their home equity just to invest. I've seen gamblers refinance their homes every twelve months just to pay off the gambling debts they have incurred on their credit cards. With a legitimate investment opportunity, these people would be doing themselves a favor.

The key is to present an investment opportunity which creates as much excitement as it does the potential for profit. That's because as a group of prospective investors, the one thing gamblers have in common is that they are as much addicted to risk as they are to excitement. An investment opportunity which brings some magic and exhilaration into their dreary slot machine playing lives will dramatically increase the number of people who commit to your partnership.

Another thing about gamblers is that once they have financially committed to your investment, it is relatively easy to extract an escalating commitment from them. This continuing investment process is something they are very comfortable with. To them, it's not that different from remaining at the black jack table hour after hour. The effect on their brain chemistry is essentially the same. Once they're invested, they need to escalate it in order to continue feeding on the excitement.

The great thing about gamblers as investors is that if they make money, they will not only boast about it to every other gambler they know, but they will insist on bringing them in on the opportunity.

Remember that a key component in structuring an appealing investment for gamblers is risk and a substantial rate of return. They are not apt to be very interested if the offering is too conservative or conventional. The idea is to use this group to underwrite investment opportunities with a level of risk that would drive away more conservative investors.

STRIP-MINING DIVORCEES

Another gold mine of prospective investors are divorcees who reside in high income areas. Many of these women walk away with sizeable holdings after their divorce. It is a target group that is often seeking life-altering experiences to make up for the mind-numbing boredom of their recently dissolved marriage.

Depending on the zip code they reside in, this demographic of investor can often be solicited for five to six figures. They also tend to respond very favorably to female presenters who are accompanied by male experts and partners.

MILKING TRUST FUND BABIES

If you are thinking about approaching trust fund babies as potential investors, there are some things you should know. Generally speaking, this demographic tends to be dominated by two groups.

Group number one is typically extremely conservative, and very concerned about investing in anything that would compromise their ability to continue maintaining their trust fund lifestyle. If you invented a fuel injector able to get 300 miles per gallon, most of these people would still pass on that investment opportunity.

Group number two is slightly less conservative, but is surrounded with so many layers of experts and skeptics that though they may be slightly more inclined to participate in your investment, they are often talked out of it by the people around them.

Most amateurs view these groups as the Holy Grail of prospective investors, but their reluctance and risk aversion often makes them the exact opposite.

From a prospective investor standpoint, each of the above groups can represent some opportunity. Matching a suitable investment to the appropriate investor is the crucial part of the process.

SALESMANSHIP GANGSTERNOMIC STYLE

Gangsters, drug dealers, dictators and CEOs make the best salesmen on earth. No one else in the world of real estate, cars, computers, stocks or legitimate pharmaceutical sales even comes close.

If you think about the staggering importance of sales ability in our economy, and then review the sale skills possessed by some of history's great gangsters and imprisoned CEOs, you can't help but be impressed.

Drug lord Pablo Escobar possessed such incredible salesmanship that he allegedly went from selling stolen tombstones to selling cocaine in such global quantities that it began to affect the gross national product of Columbia.

Al Capone's salesmanship of alcohol during prohibition was in part driven by such extraordinary sales skills that he was allegedly handling more cash flow than several Fortune 500 companies.

Whether it's the ability of a deranged and homicidal gangster to convince an innocent small town girl to date him, or his ability to convince an entire continent to purchase a white powdery substance he manufactures in rat-infested huts down in the jungle, the salesmanship these people possess is extraordinary.

There are some salesmanship qualities shared by both gangsters and CEOs alike. Here are just a few you may wish to make note of:

Gangster Charisma – Effective gangsters and CEOs both seem to possess a degree of charisma that allows them to sell very effectively. If you study charisma at this level, you will notice it often manifests itself in an ability to make locked and unblinking eye contact with the person you're selling to, while projecting a harmonic quality in your voice that implicitly conveys honesty.

Liking Someone You Distrust – This is a fascinating phenomenon which has been reported and observed in countless victims of scams. When interviewed by police after they have been scammed, victims will often report liking the con man so much. they deliberately ignored their instinctive distrust of him. There are also many incidents where the victim was so fond of the person who stole from them that they felt guilty about reporting them to the police. Great criminal salesmen seem to be able to generate so much likability that it tends to blind people.

A Sociopathic Ability To Lie – This also seems to be a very common characteristic amongst CEOs and great gangsters. You have no doubt seen it countless times during televised trials of corrupt corporate heads, as well as criminals being tried for capital crimes. There is that complete absence of any sign of remorse or guilt while they are selling or testifying. It's almost as though they have consciously shut down the emotional center of their brain during this process.

Deadly Charm – This trait seems to be almost universally possessed by great gangster salesmen. If you perform a visual analysis of charming behavior, it appears rooted in two elements. The first is the maintenance of an ongoing smile during conversation. That alone seems to have a disarming effect. The second element is usually the presence of power or physical attractiveness. Either one of these will magnify the amount of charm someone is capable of projecting.

A Percentage Of Truth – Last but not least is the ability of great criminal and corporate salesmen to sprinkle their pitch with enough truth to suspend the buyer's disbelief. The more you sprinkle, the easier the sale. A truly masterful sales pitch will be drenched in so much truth, charm and charisma that it causes the client to slip into a buyer's trance. It's a thing of beauty to behold.

Criminal Business Model *Extraordinary salesmanship is a minimal prerequisite for embarking on any criminal enterprise.*

GangsterNomic Legitimate Business Model Alternative *Extraordinary salesmanship is a minimal prerequisite for leadership in any corporate enterprise. The one thing to remember before embarking on any major sales presentation is that you are not there to sell—you are there to create magic and awe. You are there to reach deep into their souls and connect with that part of them that wants to be inspired by wondrous opportunities. You are there to be their father and their savior. Most importantly, you're there to show them the "way".*

CLOSING A BIG DEAL GANGSTERNOMIC STYLE

One problem which confronts every salesperson, professional marketer or negotiator is the occasional need to close a huge deal that just seems impossible.

The objections to closing that deal may be conventional or extraordinary, but what matters is that you are able to get to the finish line.

What follows are some suggested tips that can be used under a variety of circumstances. Some of them are unique, some are subtle, and some will blow the client away. What's important is that you apply them to a sales circumstance that is appropriate.

Close The Deal On A Private Jet – This technique works best as a reward for those clients who have already agreed to close. High-end salespeople will often throw in a trip to Vegas on a private jet to celebrate the closing of a very substantial deal. There is something about being aboard a private jet that just screams "this is how life was meant to be lived". Having clients accompany you on a jet creates an aura of success that is difficult to forget the next time they're in a buying mood.

Close The Deal On A Yacht – Not as impactful as closing the deal on a private jet, but more affordable and quite impressive in its own right. Once again, due to the obvious cost involved, this tactic should be used as more of a reward for a deal whose closing is a foregone conclusion.

Talk To Previous Clients – Allow a hesitant new client to speak with several of your previous satisfied clients if you think that may convince them to close the deal.

Offer Them Something More Important Than Cost – Sometimes an important deal can be closed by offering the client something more important than the lowest price. If you can offer the client the ability to leapfrog a competitor by offering them "first to market" status with a new product or service, that may allow them to capture so much of an early market share advantage that it's worth more than anything else to them.

Reduced Price Renewal Guarantee – Psychologically speaking, this is a very powerful contractual clause as well as an incentive to close. What these clauses typically say is that when it's time to do business with you again, by renewing our contract we "guarantee your next contractual price will be lower than your current price". You can only offer this guarantee if you have done a significant analysis of your projected future costs and profits, and are completely certain this is possible. Including this type of clause dramatically increases your ability to retain clients, but it is also imperative that the clause be written very carefully.

PREDATORY RAINMAKERS

Rainmakers are people with a great talent for bringing in high-end clients. Different industries give them different titles, but they all serve the same function which is to generate more business.

What often happens is that someone with a significant client list or contact database will be hired by a company to generate business. Sometimes it is effective, and other times it simply runs dry. The reason is that rainmakers only stick around as long as they think their client base isn't substantial enough to support them exclusively. The minute they hit that point of independence, the rainmaker quits and goes into business for himself.

The GangsterNomic approach to rainmaking is quite different. Rather than hiring people who are able to bring in new business, what you should do instead is hire people who are capable of breaking business away from a competitor. That sort of predatorial rainmaking is extremely effective if properly executed.

Instead of paying them a modest percentage of the business they generate, you should pay them a very aggressive first year percentage, and then taper it off on subsequent years for existing accounts. This provides the kind of inducement that competitors would find very difficult to turn down. If someone is making three percent at their current place of employment, and you offer them fifteen to bring a client over to you, it's going to prove very difficult to refuse.

Another aspect of predatory rainmaking is that it is far more cost effective than attempting to generate new business. Listed below are some rainmaker options:

Eastern European Ex-Presidents – If you are attempting to generate business in any of the Eastern European bloc countries, then you can retain the services of an ex-president, or even a current cabinet member, for a fraction of what such lobbying services would cost when hiring his U.S. counterpart.

Former American Presidential Candidates – Hiring a former Presidential candidate to act as your firm's rainmaker will not only generate great contacts, but it will also result in your organization receiving substantial press.

Retired U.S. Astronauts – You would be surprised at how many people are more impressed by a man who has walked on the moon than they are by a politician. They also have the added benefit of being slightly more affordable.

Senior Vice President Of Sales / Marketing – Successfully hiring this person away from your competitor is likely to impact them very severely if the person brings significant accounts over to your company.

Another thing to remember about predatory rainmaking is that you should not limit your efforts to North America. Offshore companies have spent the last two decades coming to the United States and hiring some of our most gifted talent. There is absolutely no reason you shouldn't feel free to reciprocate by going after the talent and major accounts of companies located offshore.

In many instances, it may actually be easier financially and logistically to go after the clients and employees of a foreign competitor. Cash offers speak very loudly overseas, and are usually more than welcome if presented intelligently.

GANGSTER MARKETING VERSUS MADISON AVENUE MARKETING

Whenever you see a major boiler room operation trying to sell phony land deals in Florida, free vacation trips to the Caribbean, or diet and weight loss pills that will also enhance your sexual stamina, they tend to get marketed in very innovative ways.

Back in the '70s and '80s, scams would be marketed with very seductive phone pitches designed to erode your reluctance to purchase. No matter what your objection, the scammer at the other end of the phone would have a scripted response designed to overcome it.

That business model evolved into one in which boiler room operators where replaced with very slick and impressive video tapes or DVDs designed to seduce you with displays of all the wealth you'd be able to enjoy if you just found the courage within yourself to invest in this latest opportunity.

As the production values and marketing techniques of criminal organizations evolved, an interesting development began to arise. It became apparent that the approach and sophistication of their marketing efforts began to converge with those of legitimate corporate marketers. Essentially, the marketing methodologies of these two worlds began to take on a strangely similar approach. They both seemed headed towards a gray area of marketing that can best be described as transitional. Just take a look at some of the ways these two worlds have begun to intersect their efforts and product lines:

Pornographic Marketing – Pornography used to be the purview of organized crime. It was once produced, marketed and distributed by criminals through peep shows, mail order and run-down theaters in the rat-infested parts of town. Today, pornography is distributed and sold by

Fortune 500 companies through their own satellite or cable networks. Porn stars promote their websites and email monthly newsletters with their latest product offerings. You don't even need a trench coat to see a dirty movie these days. Major hotel chains will allow you to pick up a remote control and purchase a porno movie without you ever having to get out of bed. When it comes to promoting pornography, the electronic marketing and promotional efforts of organized crime and legitimate corporate America are virtually indistinguishable. Artistically, technically and logistically, one is just as sophisticated as the other.

Drug Marketing – Yet another perfect example of how the marketing efforts of organized crime and the legitimate corporate world have converged. The sale of drugs was something that, just a few short years ago, neither gangsters nor CEOs would condone the open advertising of. It was considered bad for business on so many levels. Within the last few years, both worlds have dramatically escalated their involvement in the advertising and sale of legitimate pharmaceuticals. Some major drug corporations have begun booking commercial air time on just about any television program they think senior citizens watch. The airwaves have been flooded with drug ads designed to appeal to any human being that has ever been sick in their entire lives. Organized crime loves this because they're making mountains of money on the counterfeit pharmaceuticals they sell to unsuspecting drug store chains—counterfeit drugs which often possess little or no medical efficacy. When these counterfeit pharmaceuticals are marketed to the drug store chains and Internet drug companies by organized crime, the promotional material they employ is just as polished as the legitimate presentations made by the authentic drug company reps.

Gambling Marketing – It wasn't too long ago that gambling was something that degenerates had to fly to Las Vegas to do in secret with their mistresses. Many casinos were controlled by organized crime syndicates which hated cameras. Today, gambling is one of the most heavily promoted industries in the country. Many state governments spend millions of dollars each year to promote their own lottery. Some casinos advertise so heavily that they have given rise to boutique ad agencies that specialize in gaming promotion.

What's interesting about the legitimate world of Madison Avenue's recent advertising campaigns is that they are pushing the envelope almost as aggressively as some criminal organizations are.

Here's a perfect example: many con men in the past have observed their intended victims for some time before stinging them with a con of some sort; the intent being to learn as much about a mark as possible before you hit him for money. Information just makes the process that much easier.

Today, major corporations and advertisers will plant programs on your computer called "cookies". They can track, record and transmit almost anything you do on your computer to their advertising client. The client receives this information over the Internet and then automatically sends you a marketing pitch that is perfectly suited for you as an individual.

If a gangster had snuck into your home and planted a listening device to record you discussing personal information, it would be considered a major felony. Yet when it is done over the Internet by a group of people who may want information equally as personal, it's considered marketing.

HEMORRHAGE MARKETING

Hemorrhage marketing is one of those dirty little secrets that none of the professionals in the world of advertising, marketing, public relations or politics like to discuss. They avoid discussing it because publicly they like to present themselves as being above that sort of behavior.

The reality is, many of them have made millions of dollars with hemorrhage marketing, and will continue to do so whenever another opportunity presents itself.

Hemorrhage marketing is a phenomenon where advertisers or public relations representatives spot a competitor of one of their clients that is in serious trouble. They may be suffering from product tampering, allegations of corporate fraud, political misbehavior, or some other catastrophic event that threatens their very corporate or political existence.

They will immediately assemble a group that is tasked with creating a marketing or public relations campaign that will allow their client to benefit from his competitor's newfound weakness. These groups are typically tasked with two immediate goals. One is to help their client financially exploit his competitor's weakness, and the other is to design the campaign in a way that does not appear to be hemorrhage marketing.

Everyone wants to exploit their competitor's weakness, but no one wants to look like a bottom-feeding vulture in the process. Great painstaking efforts will be taken to mask these campaigns with sympathetic and helpful qualities its creators hope will conceal their true intent—an intent which is always designed to stick the dagger into the back of the competitor while he's still vulnerable.

Just watch what happens the next time you see a politician or major corporation in trouble. You will see a flurry of ads which miraculously and coincidentally appear out of thin air in an effort to help the victim's constituents or customers see things in a light that is more favorable to a competitor.

These are some of the most artfully produced and executed campaigns in the industry. Properly timed, they are capable of doing more damage in a single week than years of conventional advertising will do.

AMBUSH ADVERTISING

This is another fairly new GangsterNomic tactic that has been employed a great deal by companies and their ad agencies. It is very popular because it sucker-punches the competition while at the same time allowing your company to benefit from the millions of dollars they've spent on their own ads.

Here's how it works: a competitor of yours is going to be debuting a major product or service. They have spent millions of dollars in advertising and promotion to call attention to the upcoming launch date of their new product. Television ads, radio, print and electronic promotions are lighting up all across the media globe in an effort to make sure that everyone knows that, on such-and-such date, their new product is set to conquer the marketplace.

One week before their product launch date, your company launches a competing product and advertising campaign designed to steal their thunder. Now all the analysts, critics and reporters who have been primed to do a story on your competitor's product will undoubtedly mention yours as well. This is great because it allows you to ride the enormous and expensive media wave that was paid for by your competitor. And, if your product is genuinely superior, then many of the reviewers or critics who do stories on the other product will feel obligated to mention the superiority of yours.

It's as GangsterNomic as GangsterNomic gets when it comes to corporate opportunism; and, best of all, it works.

INCENTIVIZING CORPORATE DISHONESTY

In organized crime, the incentive for dishonesty has usually been money. The more you lied, cheated or stole, the more wealth you accumulated. In the corporate sector, things are a little more complex. The incentives for dishonesty are there; they just tend to be disguised or misrepresented in ways that never cease to amaze. Here are some great examples of incentivized dishonesty:

Warranties – The sale of meaningless extended warranties by manufacturers and retailers has become such an impressive display of deception, ambiguity and misrepresentation, that it causes one to marvel at how severely they can distort the English language. The only thing more creative than the language of most extended warranties are the lengths most service departments will go to deny any subsequent claim for warranty coverage. Most of the salespeople who sell these extended warranties know they're a joke; however, that never prevents them from collecting a commission.

Advancing Obsolescence – This is a design and manufacturing paradigm that says each new model of your product should have a life span that is slightly shorter than its predecessor, but not so much shorter that it alienates the consumer and destroys their brand loyalty. As most honest manufacturing engineers will tell you behind closed doors, designing a product that lasts too long is a great way to lose your job. This is a paradigm that has taken products that were once considered permanent or long-term purchases, and made them temporary or even disposable. Some of the products or services which have fallen into the category over the last decade include cameras, clothing, road repairs, and stereos. The reasons these activities can be described as dishonest is that, while many products are being designed to last for shorter periods of time, they are simultaneously being designed to look sturdier and longer-lasting.

These are just a few examples of how consumers have come to pay a premium for the privilege of being lied to during the sales process.

HOW TO WIN FRIENDS AND HUMILIATE
CORPORATE COMPETITORS

Hemorrhage marketing, performed at its best, is an art form that looks more like an act of compassionate corporate humanitarianism than the highly opportunistic predatory behavior that it truly is. Properly executed, it should capture as many of your wounded competitor's clients as possible, while making it appear as though you are simply trying to help in a time of crisis.

One of the tactics involves avoiding any inference of blame or condemnation, and instead providing a helpful option which you hope will assist your competitor's clients in their darkest hour of need.

You have a competitor whose sports utility vehicles are rolling over and killing people in record numbers? Perhaps people should know that your vehicles have a much wider and more stable wheelbase. Is a competitor's off-the-shelf medicine being opened and tampered with by criminals attempting to poison the public? Maybe people should know how tamper-resistant your medicine bottles are. Maybe you should run commercials to that effect in very large numbers while this crisis is developing? These are some of the gentler hypothetical scenarios. More aggressive examples occur every month, and result in ad campaigns that cost millions but generate hundreds of millions in revenues.

AFTER YOU'VE DESTROYED A COMPETITOR

Destroying a competitor is only the precursor to the final stages of competition. After you have driven them out of business, you begin to acquire their assets at below market cost and go after their client base. It is really the acquisition of their assets and client base that seals the fate of your competition.

If too much acrimony hasn't developed, then another element to all of this is the hiring of some of their key employees. They tend to be the greatest assets of your competitor anyway.

Properly executed in an atmosphere free of emotion and sentiment, the act of defeating a competitor and then acquiring its assets is about as GangsterNomic as it gets outside the real jungle.

Criminal Business Model *In the criminal world, once you have eliminated a competitor, the last thing criminals usually do is dispose of his remains.*

GangsterNomic Legitimate Business Model Alternative *In the corporate world, eliminating a competitor is usually followed by efforts to acquire his assets and client base.*

THE ENEMY OF MY ENEMY IS MY SILENT BUSINESS PARTNER

In the world of organized crime, if you are dealing with an extraordinarily powerful competitor, it is common to form an alliance with his enemy so that the two of you can pool your resources in an effort to defeat him. Gang wars over drug territories often erupt when the balance of power shifts because of a new alliance that has formed between two minor gangs uniting to take on a major adversary.

In the corporate world, there was a classic example of this several years ago when dozens of smaller software companies united in their effort to assist the U.S. government's anti-trust battle against one of the largest software companies in the world.

Forming a coalition like this can be both dangerous and lifesaving for a business. The majority of them are not only silent but extremely secretive. They will exchange information, resources and sometimes even political assistance, all while remaining in the shadows for as long as possible.

Some such unions may even be completely passive, involving little more than an informal agreement not to compete with each other in a manner that would only help their much larger common enemy.

If you follow their natural progression in both the corporate and criminal world, you will see that when they succeed, these loosely formed coalitions eventually become powerful cartels. When they reach that level, their sole purpose will be to protect whatever market they have cultivated and help foster its growth. Criminal and business cartels tend to become almost organic in their ability to defend themselves and all that they've created. In many instances, their power and influence even rivals those of the governments that are supposed to oversee them.

All business advantages aside, there is another interesting psychological phenomenon that occurs when two organizations unite to combat a common enemy. It's a strange multiplier effect that seems to provide the two forces joining together with more psychological and economic fortitude than one would expect. Psychologically, it is almost as if one plus one somehow equals three under these extreme circumstances. These bonds can be as effective as they are productive. Unfortunately, if they are too powerful, they will eventually give rise to the birth of a new alliance designed to defeat them.

SURVEILLANCE-BASED MARKETING

This is an area of marketing that will only continue to grow. At the moment, computer "cookies" are tracking and recording much of what transpires on your computer.

Surveillance-based marketing has already migrated to other areas of your life. The grocery store you shop at probably uses your discount shopping card to track what you're purchasing so that they can then email you flyers of similar products going on sale next month.

Many banks now monitor your account activity to determine what sort of investment and savings opportunity they should pitch to you.

Some casinos are now placing tracking devices into each and every gaming chip you bet with to determine your hourly rate of play. Computers can calculate the exact moment at which a representative should be sent over to your table to offer you a larger room or a free meal, so as to encourage additional play from you.

Insurance companies are building massive databases of your medical history and pharmaceutical needs, so that they can more accurately assess you as a future claims risk.

The kind of monitoring activity that was once considered unsavory or illegal is now considered an absolute necessity by the most aggressive criminals and CEOs.

Criminal Business Model *Surveilling a future target of your criminal activity was once referred to as "casing". Today a simple computer check can tell someone more about their intended victim than a week of sitting in some van with a pair of binoculars ever could.*

GangsterNomic Legitimate Business Model Alternative
The legitimate computerized gathering of detailed

information about prospective clients is called "data mining". It is a business practice engaged in by thousands of companies each year, and is a recognized tool in every modern marketer's belt. Some of the better database companies can data mine a specific individual and tell you everything from the movies they like to purchase to what size pants they wear.

25 SIMILARITIES SHARED BY HIGH-LEVEL GANGSTERS AND CEOS

To provide you with a better business understanding of the gangster / CEO psyche, I am going to describe some of their profile similarities. Seeing these will allow you to understand their decision making tendencies.

1) Both will employ media experts to generate publicity for those good deeds they hope will cause the public to forget the negative things they've done.

2) Most employees and subordinates are seen by both as being completely disposable and interchangeable.

3) They never make a contract they haven't already determined how to break.

4) They always assume that their competition is at least as devious and calculating as they are.

5) They will often employ the same lawyers and CPAs.

6) They both have a tendency to manipulate their organization's accounting statements for their own advantages.

7) Gangsters and CEOs often insulate themselves from the repercussions of potentially compromising decisions by having their subordinates execute them.

8) When convicted, both will request incarceration at the same minimum security prisons.

9) Both tend to maintain personal bank accounts at the same Swiss, Liechtenstein, Cayman Island, Gibraltar, Panama and Isle of Man banks.

10) CEOs and gangsters tend to both spend considerable sums on lobbyists.

11) Both will pay for the companionship of celebrities so that they can be photographed with them to elevate their own media profile.

12) Both will reach out to the Lord and find religion minutes after they are indicted.

13) Some of the most successful CEOs and gangsters have never received college degrees.

14) As unlikely as it sounds, both often tend to love the companionship of controlling women.

15) Most CEOs and gangsters seldom carry cash.

16) Both are often very reluctant to put controversial or potentially compromising decisions on paper.

17) They will often retain the services of the same tailors, jewelers, hair stylists, real estate agents, financial advisors, personal trainers, landscaping companies and surveillance experts.

18) A high percentage of gangsters and CEOs live within three miles of each other in the same four communities. They are Manhattan, Beverly Hills, Palm Beach, and Boca Raton.

19) They often frequent the same top five restaurants and nightclubs in each of the above cities.

20) Most of them will employ the services of the same fractional jet ownership companies.

21) They tend to hire their lieutenants and vice presidents because they are non-threatening. You almost never see them surrounded by people whose IQ or ambition exceeds their own. This failure to surround themselves with greatness is often the Achilles heel of both.

22) Tactically, they both tend to conduct business in a manner that can be described as strategic.

23) Both tend to view adversity as opportunity.

24) Each would much rather have his subordinates fear them than respect them.

25) Gangsters and CEOs tend to view infidelity the same way they view business. To them, it is purely recreational and utterly devoid of any moral or ethical component. If pressed behind closed doors, most would acknowledge that they view morality with the same philosophical contemptuousness that they view organized religion.

GANGSTERNOMIC CHARACTERISTICS

What do Attilla The Hun, Jesse James , Pablo Escobar, Al Capone, Sam Giancana, Meyer Lansky, Lucky Luciano, Dutch Schultz and Bugsy Siegel have in common?

1) Not one of the above men was ever reported to have graduated with an advanced degree in business or finance from a university.

2) Not one of them ever had to file bankruptcy, or was ever publicly reported to have needed the assistance of an investment counselor.

3) Each of the above men's personal net worth grew at a rate that not only far exceeded the average growth rate of the Fortune 500 firms in existence during their lifetimes, but they also retained stewardship and control of their companies or organizations much longer than the average corporate CEO retains his job.

4) Not one of them was ever publicly reported to have used a resume, headhunter, career counselor or job placement office to obtain a job.

5) None of them was ever publicly reported to have ever collected unemployment.

6) Each of the above men amassed real estate holdings more significant than many of the real estate experts of their day.

EMPLOYING COUNTERSURVEILLANCE TECHNOLOGY

Just a few years ago in the Colombian City of Cali, a special team of soldiers dedicated to fighting narcotics was reported to have broken into an upscale condo. What they found was so incredible that it stunned both them and intelligence organizations all across the globe. The condo contained a multimillion-dollar IBM mainframe computer that was manned by half a dozen technicians at all times. It was similar to those used by major financial institutions.

This was such an incredible development that the Columbian government authorized the DEA to fly the computer back to the United States, where a very complex analysis of it could be made. What U.S. experts found rocked them to their very core.

The computer was found to have contained a database with the personal phone numbers of American diplomats and agents who worked in Columbia. Even more startling was the fact that the computer contained all the phone log files originating from the Cali phone company. It also had a highly specialized program that allowed it to perform data mining, a high-tech process which cross-references all the phone calls made in Cali with the known phone numbers of Colombian law enforcement, intelligence officers and cartel personnel. This meant that the computer was performing an ongoing automated hunt for phone number matches to see who in the cartel may have been leaking information over the phone to law enforcement. Whenever the computer found a match that fingered an informant, the cartel responded very quickly and violently.

The cartel was also reported to be doing some other very interesting things. For instance, in order to maximize the chance of their drug planes making it to their destinations undetected, the cartel mapped out the radar sweeps of drug surveillance planes. Once they knew the radar sweep patterns, they could plan their flight paths accordingly.

Another countersurveillance technique used by the cartel was a move away from the transmission of voice messages toward a greater reliance on digital messages. Digital messages can be broken up into segments and transmitted at high frequencies over a radio network that is extremely difficult to intercept and decipher once the information is encrypted.

These are very extreme examples of the sort of criminal countersurveillance techniques employed in the late '90s. What they reveal is the importance that these groups placed on the preservation of their proprietary information.

What's interesting is that many companies in the legitimate business world will budget millions of dollars a year for catering, executive travel by jet and limousine, as well as the maintenance of corporate hospitality suites at major sports arenas and stadiums. What few of them realize is that a security team hired by one of their competitors can aim a fairly inexpensive laser microphone at the window overlooking their boardroom meetings and hear every word that is said. Every discussion about new products, budgets, problems, etc., can all be recorded, converted into a computer file and emailed across the globe within minutes of the actual conversation taking place.

Corporate competitors can use this information to make money on several levels. First, they can use it to obtain a strategic advantage. If you know your competitor's strategy, then you can adjust for it in real time. The second is that the inside information can be used to conduct highly leveraged stock market trades that can pay off very aggressively.

LIVE BY THE SCRAMBLER... DIE BY THE SCRAMBLER

The ubiquity of cell phones has given businesspeople a false sense of security—a feeling that they are somehow more secure on a cell phone than a cordless phone.

If you remember nothing else from GangsterNomics, you should always remember this: all cell phone conversations can be intercepted and recorded.

If you are going to conduct any sensitive business on a cell phone whatsoever, then you must use a scrambler. If the information you're discussing has any serious economic value, you must use a scrambler. If you would hate to see whatever you're discussing on the news or in a tabloid, then use a scrambler.

Don't be misled into thinking that it is unlikely to happen because it's illegal. Making it illegal just means that the people who do this sort of thing for a living get to charge more for their services.

If you conduct business in a foreign city which is also the capital of its country, then the likelihood of your cell phone conversation being compromised just went up 500%. Foreign capitals tend to contain a large number of embassies, and under those circumstances everyone is electronically monitoring everyone else. Chances are, your cell phone is being monitored by both the host country and several of the embassies in your area.

Criminal Business Model Criminal organizations place a great premium on both preserving the security of their own information, as well as obtaining the secrets of their competitors. Spending five percent of their adjusted gross for security and countersurveillance that will keep some guy with a chainsaw out of their bedroom late at night is regarded as a stellar investment.

GangsterNomic Legitimate Business Model Alternative The countersurveillance efforts of most major companies are limited to putting a firewall on their computer system and hiring someone to come in each week and perform bulk shredding of their sensitive documents. If they really consider themselves proactive, they will hire some company to monitor Internet blogs for sensitive information on them. That is a huge display of short-sightedness. A more aggressive GangsterNomic strategy involving actively pursuing knockoff counterfeiters in Eastern Europe and Asia will pay greater dividends. The Business Software Alliance and the Motion Picture Association of America have embarked on a Herculean effort to thwart software and movie piracy in all four corners of the globe. This is the kind of proactive business model and effort a company needs in order to curb the success of competitors who cross the legal line. It is also extremely important to scramble your sensitive cell phone conversations. You can perform a search on the Internet using the keywords "cell phone scramblers", and you will locate a number of companies which sell this technology.

KEEPING THE BODIES BURIED

All organizations need to maintain the confidentiality of information that may compromise them. In the criminal world, it means information related to the commission of crimes, but in corporate America it may mean much more.

On a GangsterNomic level, there is a heightened need for corporations to safeguard or destroy information related to fraud, technological innovations, accounting issues, strategic plans, and product information. The need to safeguard this information is greater than ever given the success that corporate competitors, government agencies and plaintiff's attorneys are having in obtaining it using both legal and illegal means.

Some of the tactics and technology that are becoming more commonly used amongst criminals and corporations to safeguard their secrets are as follows:

Self-Destructive Email – This is an email program that allows people to write and send emails which will self-destruct and disappear after they have been opened and read by their intended recipient.

Countersurveillance Systems – Most of the offices of CEOs and gangsters now contain countersurveillance equipment that will prevent someone with a recording device on their person from taping the conversation without their knowledge. Many of the offices also have acoustic jammers and bug sweepers. At this level, it is often viewed as an inconvenient cost of doing business.

Document Shredding – Document shredders have become the new must-have office item for anyone concerned about corporate espionage or litigation. Crosscut shredders tend to be more effective. Make certain to use a shredder that can also destroy CDs, DVDs and diskettes.

Communications Protocols – Most gangsters and CEOs now have very specific communication protocols which instruct everyone in their organization never to discuss sensitive information over the phone, fax, email, as well as by written memo. The new mandate is, if it can be even remotely interpreted by an attorney as illegal or actionable, then under no circumstances should it ever be committed to a formal communiqué. Messages like these should always be communicated face-to-face, and in an oblique and cryptic manner designed to make their intent questionable. When conveyed face-to-face, there should never be a third party present that could act as a witness. Oblique language like this was first made popular by drug dealers decades ago when they attempted to discuss business without revealing specifics. A far more polished version of it is now so common in the corporate world that once innocent words like "issue" can now mean anything from accounting fraud to pending indictment.

With this level of paranoia, it is only a matter of time before someone in law enforcement or organized crime starts a mobile document shredding company for the sole purpose of surreptitiously obtaining sensitive documents from a competitor or criminal suspect.

LITIGATION – GANGSTERNOMIC STYLE

One great new television show in development is called **Godfather Court** (see **www.Godfathercourt.com**). It is a next generation comedic reality show in which real people litigate real cases in front of a panel of judges comprised of actors and actresses who have played gangsters and criminals in movies. Unlike real court cases where people pretend to tell the truth, on Godfather Court, people will be encouraged to lie as pathologically as possible in order to win their cases.

While developing the show, it became clear that litigation was like an unexploded nuclear device. The threat of using

184

it is almost as powerful as its actual use. Great litigators have a few things in common with successful gangsters:

1) Both love to collect damaging information about their opponents before they go into battle with them.

2) They love to ignore the rules of war. This is especially true of major litigation firms.

3) Gangsters and litigators almost never concede final defeat.

4) Both love to buy judges. Gangsters put money in a brown bag and slip it under someone's door, while litigators will contribute to a judge's re-election campaign.

5) Each enjoys the war more than the outcome.

Here are some GangsterNomic Litigation categories that seam to be growing in popularity:

Extortive Litigation – This is a very common category in which a deep pocket plaintiff will sue a financially weaker adversary in the hopes that the cost of litigation will drive them to surrender.

Patent Broadside Litigation – Also a fast growing sector. Here you will find that someone who owns a patent for a certain technology or business model will attempt to seize the patent rights of another individual by going to court to broaden the definition and scope of their patent so widely that it infringes upon or completely obviates the rights of the patent holder they're suing. These cases are often determined not by the interpretation of the original patent applications, but more by the financial and legal strength of the litigants.

Cease And Desist Letter – This is one of the most cost-effective legal tools in the arsenal when going up against a defendant with nominal resources. It shows up in your mailbox like a smoldering grenade that's threatening to go off. You open it, and inside is a letter on some law firm's stationary that contains the names of as many as one hundred lawyers running down both margins. The cease and desist letter basically tells you to stop whatever your doing or they will sue. The huge laundry list of lawyer names is designed to intimidate you.

PURCHASING THE TRUTH

Litigation, like all other areas of commerce, has become a market-driven phenomenon. Since one's ability to prevail in court is supposed to be determined by the facts, an entire industry of experts has been created to help you purchase those facts.

Members of the bar have access to an enormous list of experts for hire in every conceivable field of law and commerce. You can now bring in an accredited and acknowledged expert who will provide expertise designed to back up whatever your case requires.

Need an expert to testify that the length of the car tire skid marks in your accident would be indicative of negligence? That expert is only a phone call away. Need another expert to testify that those same car tire skid marks were made by a driver who appears to have been very diligent and in full compliance with the law? That expert witness probably has a website that is only a mouse click away.

Most major cases have become theatrical staging areas for the dueling performances of experts who have each been paid very handsomely to provide their interpretation of the facts.

Criminal Business Model *Gangsters will often bribe a witness to testify favorably in court. It is a commonly used tool for obtaining innocent verdicts.*

GangsterNomic Legitimate Business Model Alternative
Business litigants will often flood a courtroom with competing expert witnesses, each of which has been paid to testify in a manner that advances the likelihood that his client will receive a favorable verdict.

GANGSTER CONTRACTS

Did you ever wonder why there are no publicly reported or acknowledged written contracts between major criminals or their organizations? It has little to do with their fear of a paper trail or reluctance to get involved in high-profile litigation. The truth of the matter is that most criminals don't bother with written contracts because they understand how little any of that nonsense has to do with real justice. Even more importantly, they understand how much more expedient the threat of violence is when compared to long-term litigation.

The first GangsterNomic rule of contract law is that they should always include multiple escape clauses. If possible, those clauses should also penalize the other party whenever you need to exit the agreement.

The second rule of GangsterNomic contract law is that the agreement should always include penalties for ongoing litigation that is contrary to your interests.

The third rule of Gangsternomic contract law is that the deal should always include incentives for adherence to the terms. This way you can penalize them when they get out of hand, and reward them when they tow the line.

FIVE BRASS KNUCKLE LITIGATION TECHNIQUES

If you are confronted with a litigation-prone adversary that has his lawyers coming after you with both barrels blazing, there are some GangsterNomic tactics you can consider:

Videotape The Deposition – It only costs a few hundred dollars more, but if you videotape the deposition you can then post video clips of some of the embarrassing questions they had to answer on the internet. If it is particularly juicy, you can call up the media and have them broadcast the video on the air. This isn't going to win your case for you, but it will show the other side that you're clever enough to draw first blood early in the fight. Make certain to get your lawyer's pre-approval on this.

Hire A Private Detective To Surveil The CEO Of Their Company – The point here is not to try and dig up dirt that probably won't be admitted into court. The point here is to demonstrate that you are taking the legal offensive. If your private investigator can make his presence known to their CEO during an inauspicious or potentially compromising moment, all the better. Make certain to get your lawyer's pre-approval on this.

Meet With The Competitors Of The Company You're Involved In Litigation With – The point here is to determine if the two of you have any common legal ground or information that may be of benefit to each other. Make certain to get your lawyer's pre-approval on this.

Media Coverage – Determine if there are any public policy or broader issues in your case that would affect the public at large. If so, the media is far more apt to take an interest in covering your case. Make certain to get your lawyer's pre-approval on this.

Disgruntled Ex-Employees / Vendors / Business Partners – Have your private investigator locate any disgruntled ex-employees / venders / business partners who may have useful information. These people are worth their weight in litigation gold. Even better are the former spouses and ex-girlfriends of some of these people, because they tend not to be bound by non-disclosure agreements. Make certain to get your lawyer's pre-approval on this.

Gangsters love seeking out the disgruntled employees of their enemies. South American drug cartels are famous for spending vast sums of money on the information acquired from such sources.

SELECTING A WARTIME CONSIGLIERE

As any gangster will tell you the most important decision you can make in wartime is having the right "consigliere". That's the Italian word for an adviser or counselor to an organized crime family. Who advises you before, during and after a major conflict often determines whether the crime family lives or dies.

The same is true of corporate legal battles. Selecting the right lead counsel prior to a major legal battle determines 90% of the outcome. Much of your selection criteria will be driven by the precise nature of your litigation, but generally speaking, here are some guidelines for selecting a wartime consigliere:

Major Cases – If your case is one with national ramifications, or one that perhaps poses a threat to the economic future of you or your corporation, then you need a law firm with two things. First, it must have an extraordinary reputation for aggressive and tenacious litigation skills. Secondly, the firm you select must be politically connected. At this level you need to choose a firm which not only engages in lobbying on a national level, but also one that has unbridled access to decision-makers in both government and the media.

Mid-Level Cases – If your case is one which doesn't possess any national component or the ability to financially destroy your firm, but would still cause significant economic damage, then you need to select a law firm with tremendous negotiation and settlement skills. The majority of such cases end up settled, and you want to make certain the terms are as favorable as possible.

Small Cases – If you are an individual or a small business owner involved in litigation that is serious, then you want to consider hiring an attorney who lives and breathes litigation. You want someone who is both hyperaggressive and extremely tenacious, not someone who simply goes through the motions because he intends to settle this as quickly as possible so that he can make money. You want a litigator who, for all intents and purposes, appears to the other side to live and breath conflict and litigation. Attorneys like this are typically very athletic and motivated. Stay away from your city's legal media star. This is the attorney who is running ads on TV every 15 minutes. These guys will usually sign on to your case and then turn it over to someone else thirty seconds after you leave the office. You want your case handled by the attorney you selected, not his referral.

FIRING YOUR ATTORNEY

Litigation can drag on for years. Sometimes during the course of a case, it becomes apparent that your attorney is either not addressing your needs very aggressively or he is just incompetent. There are so many incompetent attorneys out there that I'm surprised someone hasn't started a website which tracks their win/loss ratios and then assigns ratings to them the same way we do to automobiles, restaurants or hospitals.

Before you fire an attorney, you have to find his replacement. Talk to friends, use an Internet search engine to do research, and then meet with several prospective attorneys. If you have done your research properly, you will usually come up with the names of three or four attorneys who everyone else in the area agrees are very good.

Meet with these guys and then hire one of them. One of the worst tactical decisions you can make in protracted litigation is sticking with an attorney who is not properly servicing your case.

ATTILA THE HUN—ORIGINAL GANGSTERNOMIC NEGOTIATOR

Whenever Attila The Hun faced the conclusion of a long battle, he had to decide on the manner in which it would end. Slaughtering the enemy would provide him with less of a kingdom to rule over. Halting the invasion prematurely would also create a false sense of confidence within his adversaries, which might pose a problem later.

To achieve an optimal solution, an adversarial situation has to be concluded at the precise moment in which doing so provides you with the most favorable terms. On the field of battle, it is usually when your opponent decides that servitude is more desirable than death. In litigation, that moment occurs when your opponent realizes that the cost of continuing will exceed the benefit of stopping.

During settlement negotiations, this moment usually occurs when your opponent decides that the likelihood of winning his remaining deal points is outweighed by the probability of the negotiations collapsing entirely.

FAILURE ARBITRAGE

This is a real growth industry that is as interesting as it is potentially lucrative from a GangsterNomic perspective. Conventional wisdom has always been that failure creates a diminished value in the marketplace. In a growing set of circumstances, this is no longer the case. In fact, the GangsterNomics view is that failure actually enhances market value in many cases. Failure arbitrage occurs when what appears to be a failing opportunity is simultaneously acquired and prepped for resale.

The easiest example of this is the entertainment industry. Here you regularly have stars and musicians with careers on the downslide. Their last couple of projects have been lackluster, and now they find their market value has dropped dramatically. Their career arc descends from movies to television to commercials, and just keeps spiraling downward. One day they are arrested for drugs or shoplifting, and suddenly their agent's phone is ringing off the hook. Offers are coming in left and right. That's a very obvious example of failure arbitrage. Now let's show you how it's done by corporate gangsters in pursuit of real money.

The first phase of failure arbitrage is to search for diminished viability. You want a to seek out a company that has sales or market share which is swirling down the drain. What the pros will do is look for a company, patent holder, or a reseller that has been adversely affected by internal forces; not externals like interest rates, fuel costs or low-cost competitors, because those are more difficult to overcome. You want internal problems like mismanagement, divorce, drug addicted CEOs, or just good old incompetence.

As the company begins to crash under the weight of its own problems, the folks involved in failure arbitrage will begin doing calculations. They run the numbers in an effort to calculate its Market Failure Value (MFV) point. This is a point in the company's diminishing market value at which its appeal as an acquisition target begins to grow. It starts growing because of the increasing number of speculators, turnaround experts and prospective buyers who are beginning to appear on the horizon, waiting for the moment to strike.

It's at that strange and contradictory point that the company's stock value decreases, while its appeal and potential sales price may actually begin to rise because of an unusual premium that gets attached to its perceived future potential.

As arbitrary as that sounds, it is even more common in the perceived valuation of people. Any sports expert will tell you that some of the best trades are made of athletes who are acquired by a sports team just after they have recovered from a major sports injury. Here the failure arbitrage is fairly straightforward. On the surface, the athlete's economic potential appears to be very diminished because of his injury. However, someone who is familiar with failure arbitrage will instinctively understand that, while one valuation of his potential is made on a superficial level causing him to appear weakened, another valuation of his recoverable future potential will reveal his true value. It is the pursuit of that hidden and recoverable value in people and companies that makes it possible to find wealth where others fail to see it.

Criminal Business Model *Criminals will often seize control of a corporation just so that they can run it into the ground, steal its inventory and then set it on fire to collect the insurance payoff. What they do is perform a very quick and instinctive failure arbitrage which reveals to them that the company will actually be worth more after they have robbed and torched it, than it would if they allowed it to continue to exist. Burning it to the ground has actually increased its value.*

GangsterNomic Legitimate Business Model Alternative *Some companies in financial difficulty actually begin to look more desirable to potential buyers the more dramatically they fail. This is because the failure arbitrage calculation potential buyers are making is not based on the rapidly diminishing stock price of the company so much as it is on the perceived turnaround value it possesses. As odd and counterintuitive as it sounds, after a certain point, failure can actually increase value.*

A GANGSTERNOMIC VIEW OF WALL STREET

The minute you begin making money, your name begins to appear on dozens of mailing and solicitation lists. You will be approached endlessly by people and organizations wanting you to invest in stocks and mutual funds.

Don't do it.

Decades ago, Al Capone was asked what he thought of investing in stocks. Capone pulled the cigar out of his mouth, started laughing and said, "Are you kidding—Wall Street? That's where the real gangsters are."

Statistically speaking, there is absolutely no difference between investing in a stock and heading down to the casino to do some gambling. The truth of the matter is that you are apt to encounter more honesty in a modern casino.

The problem with stock market investment is simply the access to information. Any information that makes its way to the public has already been factored into the stock price by the market, so it is impossible to profit from it. Not a day goes by when you don't run into some accountant or financial expert that believes he has found an undervalued stock opportunity. Some of these guys make money and some lose it, but the reality is that their profit often has little or nothing to do with their insightful analysis. More often than not, it's just plain luck or fortuitous timing.

Even the experts will acknowledge this. Have you ever wondered why, in this highly computerized era, not a single financial TV show, newspaper or magazine has ever done a five or ten-year statistical analysis of all the advice their experts have given? It is because publicly acknowledging how often they have been wrong in the past would not only be bad for ratings and circulation, but it would also compromise many of the relationships they have with Wall Street.

Think about that. We rate vehicle repair histories, hospital malpractice incidents, and aircraft failures. Newspapers and magazines will even rate the movies you see and the restaurants you eat in; but when it comes to your money, when was the last time you saw someone in the media do a long-term analysis of their own expert's financial forecasting ability?

There are guys who make millions in the market, but it's not because they're geniuses, nor is it because they are so much luckier. It's because they have access to information the guy reading the Wall Street Journal down at the corner bookstore doesn't have. That is just the way the jungle operates.

Stay out of the stock market unless you are an insider.

CRIMINAL PRICE INDEX

The criminal price index is the underworld's unofficial counterpart to all the legitimate price indexes which exist in the stock market. While it does not exist in written form for all the obvious reasons, it is just as tangible and influential.

The criminal price index is a market listing of prices for various criminal acts and services. It is broken down by region, provider, and threat level. What this means is that if you are shopping for two men capable of burglarizing a private estate on Star Island in Florida, the price of that service will be based on where the crime is committed, the caliber of people executing it, and the degree of threat involved in the crime. The threat level is usually a function of the amount of security on site combined with the quality of the police service in the jurisdiction the crime is to be committed.

What's interesting about the criminal price index is that, while it is highly informal and never reduced to writing, it is still very ubiquitous. It may be called different names in different parts of the world, but it is essentially the same everywhere you go.

It is both the determinant of market prices for criminal activity as well as the market maker for those willing to shop their services. It doesn't exist in any physical place, but it's always omnipresent and always changing. Quote someone a price for your criminal services that is too far outside the average price range for such activity, and people will pass. Quote someone a price that is too low and people will instantly assume you are an amateur that is probably too inexperienced to hire.

Another characteristic of the criminal price index is that it allows you to compare prices in various countries. Ask the right people, and you will quickly be able to determine the cost of performing a specific crime in Spain versus California.

The more sophisticated the criminals, the more research they will perform in preparation for their crime. Cost/benefit analysis of this sort is growing more common amongst white collar criminals embarking on crimes capable of netting more than a hundred thousand dollars. It's all part of the calculus.

In addition to estimating the degree of risk involved in a crime, it is also common to do an analysis of the wage costs, administrative overhead, and logistical expenses. If any one of these costs proves unacceptable, then it is common for the professionals to either relocate the crime to a more affordable country or just walk away.

CRIME BY CREDIT SCORE

There is a growing trend in which criminals select their victims based on their credit scores. This is occurring for several reasons.

As people become more sophisticated, they are downplaying their ostentatious displays of wealth by making themselves more inconspicuous and thus harder for criminals to find. That usually means driving a Toyota instead of a Mercedes, wearing little or no jewelry, and never discussing their finances.

Targeting victims by credit score makes it possible to identify them through their false veil of economic modesty.

The best way to counteract these efforts is to become even more aggressive in your efforts to project as modest a lifestyle as possible. This will help you to fly below the criminal radar, and will also make it less likely that you will be targeted by much of the random crime out there that occurs out of simple economic spite.

GANGSTERS DON'T GET SCAMMED

Not a day goes by when you don't see a story on TV or in the paper about someone getting scammed. Sometimes it is a senior citizen who loses their life savings; sometimes it's a sophisticated professional who thought it could never happen to them.

Have you ever wondered why criminals rarely try to scam other criminals? The reason for that is twofold. The first one is rather obvious in that the penalty for getting caught is usually much worse than going to jail.

The second and far more pervasive reason that gangsters and sophisticated businessmen are rarely able to scam each other is that it is very difficult to get past their radar.

All the usual scam techniques applied to Joe Sixpack tend to elicit little more than a laugh when attempted on a gangster.

Unfortunately, the techniques used by criminals and corrupt corporations are growing more sophisticated with each passing day. In light of this, we are going to equip you with a GangsterNomic skill set designed to minimize the chances of you or your company being taken advantage of by the pros.

Police Partner – This is a classic GangsterNomic technique. Here's how it works: you're approached by someone offering you a great deal on something—stocks, bonds, real estate, or used cars at bargain prices—it really doesn't matter what the scam is. As soon as they have explained all the details, you tell them that you would love to get involved but that your friend, who's a police detective, would have to come on board since the two of you are partners. Tell him that you would like to set up another meeting to introduce your friend to him so that he could hear about the investment. If your salesman shows up for meeting number two, then the odds of this investment being legitimate has just increased a bit.

Use Multiple Bank Accounts In Different Banks – We now live in a day and age when identity theft can empty your entire bank account with one keystroke. Your banks will tell you that your funds are protected, but file a claim and just watch how long the process to recoup your funds can take. You literally have to take some banks to court in identity theft cases, in order to force them to replenish your stolen funds. Most people cannot endure a five year court battle without access to their money.

The Ten Percent Rule – Never invest more than ten percent of your assets in any single investment; that includes real estate. If it goes belly-up, this limits your exposure to ten percent of your portfolio.

The Clock – Whenever someone places a deadline on an investment of any sort that seems unreasonable, simply walk away. Money talks and deadlines walk. You will always be able to find another investment. Let this one go.

Escrow With Your Attorney, Not Theirs – He who controls the escrow account controls everything. Any insistence on their part that you must use their escrow agent is usually a red flag. Just walk away.

ASSAULT ON YOUR SAVINGS

As you read this book, the savings of ordinary Americans are under such severe attack, that describing it as the electronic version of Peal Harbor would be an understatement. They are coming at people from so many different sources that victims are losing their savings in ways they can't even believe they fell for. Here are some examples that you should be on the lookout for:

Fake Product Rebate Check – One day you will open up the mail and see a $2 rebate check for some product purchase you don't recall making. The reason you don't recall making it is because you never did. This check was probably mailed to you by scamsters wanting you to deposit it into your account, so that they can get your banking information from the back of the check when it clears.

Subscription Purchase Bait And Switch – The airwaves and magazine ads have become overrun with commercials and print ads for DVDs, CDs, books and magazines that you can purchase. You place the one-time $9.95 order on your debit card, and assume that will be the end of it. The next month rolls around, and you're billed for another $9.95. You'll contact them and they will say that you've been signed up for a subscription service which will send you a new DVD or book each month. If you complain, they'll offer to cancel your subscription, but in reality, your card will continue to get billed each month. This process will go on until you cancel the card or your state's Attorney General intervenes. In very aggressive cases, the scam artists will access your bank account through your debit card and simply empty it out.

Internet Banking – Never allow your bank accounts to become Internet accessible, and don't use Internet banking websites. When you open a new account, ask your banker to disable any Internet access the account may default to. If your bank says all their accounts are Internet accessible, move to another bank or credit union. The number of illegitimate access attempts to your account being made over the Internet by both gangsters and legitimate companies is simply overwhelming. In 2005, it was publicly announced that forty million credit card numbers were hacked and stolen from an Arizona company that processes transactions for MasterCard, Discover, American Express and Visa. If that many accounts were stolen in one incident, just imagine what else is going on out there.

Multi Banking – It is extremely important that you divide your funds between at least three different banks. This way, if one account is accessed or stolen, you will still have funds in the other two accounts. Banks claim that they will cover any losses, but you will be shocked at how long and difficult the process to recover your funds from your bank may be. In some instances, you will actually have to sue your bank, which can require three to eight years of litigation before you'll see your money.

CELEBRITY BANKING SAFEGUARDS

Most people who are victimized by identity theft don't realize that if they were only afforded the same level of credit report security that celebrities are provided, it would never have happened to them.

Most of the major credit reporting agencies have special monitoring systems in place to check the activity on the accounts of celebrities and VIPs. Whenever any unusual activity is detected, they take immediate action.

If these same credit reporting agencies would allow ordinary citizens to have this same level of security monitoring and account freezing capability during an alert, much of the identity theft you now see occurring would be dramatically reduced.

FIVE PEOPLE MOST LIKELY TO DRIVE YOU INTO BANKRUPTCY

In the world of organized crime, the people who destroy you financially usually fall into two groups—the guy you tried to have killed but didn't, and someone in your organization who was recently arrested by the Feds and has now secretly become an informer for them.

In the world of business, the financial threats come from a number of directions, and can often be as difficult to see coming as a mob hit. For the most part though, here are the five people most likely to drive you into bankruptcy:

1) A disgruntled ex-wife or girlfriend who feels she is entitled to half your company and all of your child support.

2) A disgruntled former key employee who pitched you an idea you said no to, and has left to start his own company.

3) A whistleblower you should have listened to, but didn't. You tried to intimidate him with your lawyers, and now he has gone to the Feds with information you are going to regret them having.

4) A competitor's CEO with a new idea or business model that reminds you of what you used to be like when you were younger and hungrier.

5) You and your decision to prematurely rush a product to market, knowing full well it wasn't ready.

These are just a few examples; there are hundreds of others.

FIVE PEOPLE MOST LIKELY TO KEEP YOU OUT OF BANKRUPTCY

When it comes to running an organization in a financially prudent matter, there are several people that can be instrumental in keeping you out of trouble.

First and foremost, you need a great Chief Financial Officer. The best CFOs tend to be folks who come from top-tier accounting schools, and have had considerable experience turning around companies that were in financial trouble.

The next thing you need is a spouse or Vice President who is obsessed with cost-cutting. This counterbalancing influence can be especially helpful if you are predisposed to throwing money at problems.

Third on the list is a great marketing manager who can continue to help you generate the business you need to keep the revenue flowing.

Fourth on the list is a hyperaggressive sales manager who can compliment the efforts of your marketing manager. Together these two can help you reach your revenue goals despite whatever difficulties you may be facing in your business environment.

Last but not least you will need a great lawyer to help you structure your deals. Well written contracts help you secure profitable terms, and allow you to get out of trouble at a nominal cost when you need to breach them.

THE MOST DANGEROUS JOBS IN ORGANIZED CRIME

Any job in organized crime is exceedingly dangerous, but there are some which are more so than others. Here are a few jobs that peg the scale when it comes to risk and danger:

Chief Accountant And Money Launderer – Rivals may kill the mob boss without so much as batting and eye, but mob accountants and money launderers are never that lucky. When they are caught, they and their families can be tortured for weeks on end until they surrender the routing numbers, account numbers and passwords needed to get at the money.

Informer – This individual was probably caught by the Feds, and given the option of either turning informant for them or spending the rest of their life in prison. Unfortunately, being an informer and gathering information against the mob is not as easy as it use to be. The technology they now have in place to protect themselves against the unauthorized recording of their conversations is very sophisticated. Needless to say, getting caught doing so by them can have life-altering consequences.

Mob Boss – The history with these guys is long, colorful and full of abrupt endings. When the end does come, it's usually served up to them by the people who they trusted most.

THE MOST DANGEROUS JOBS IN CORPORATE AMERICA

Whistleblower – Officially everyone wants whistleblowers to be able to come forward with information on corporate wrongdoing whenever they encounter it. The politically correct position is that it will elevate the corporate bar of ethical behavior. In reality, corporate America despises whistleblowers, and will use every resource they have at their financial, legislative and judicial disposal to try and destroy them.

Executive Vice President – This is usually the lackey hired by the CEO to do all the dirty work. The EVP will get offered a nice employment contract, corner office and great-looking secretary. A year or two down the road when things get difficult, the CEO will have to make some hard decisions that are almost never ethical, and often illegal. When that happens, he'll call the EVP into his office and have a discussion with him about some policies or strategies he wants implemented. What he really means is that they are of such a sensitive nature that he can't do them himself, so the EVP will have to. There are two things you can always count on in the business world. The first is that the competition will get tougher before it gets easier. The second is that when the Federal government starts indicting everyone, you can rest assure the CEO will blame his second-in-command EVP for everything.

TOP GANGSTERNOMIC CITIES

There are a number of cities around the world which have an environment that is very conducive to GangsterNomics. By that, I mean they practice business in an ultra-aggressive and ruthless manner. Here a few of the most prominent:

Moscow, Russia – This is a city which is generating millionaires as quickly as Silicon Valley. While it is highly polarized in that most people are either extremely wealthy or very poor, what sets it apart from the rest of the world is that the tremendous risk and danger one assumes when conducting business here also makes it possible to earn vast fortunes. This is not a city that tolerates naivete or unsophistication. In fact, coming here ill-prepared will cause you to lose your money faster than you would in Vegas. But, if you are intelligent, sophisticated, well-connected, and arrive with a clever business model, then you can generate a tremendous amount of wealth. If there is any city in the world which is more preoccupied with creating wealth than New York, it has to be Moscow.

Havana, Cuba – While most Americans are prohibited from travelling to or doing business with Cuba, investors from the rest of the world are flooding in and positioning themselves for a day when the country will be free of its very old leader. When he passes away, the country's air of mystique and appeal as a tourism destination is expected to fuel tremendous growth.

Sao Paulo, Brazil – As one of the most heavily populated cities on earth, Sao Paulo has become a mecca for everyone in South America aggressively seeking opportunities.

New York – If you are plugged in and connected to the world of finance, media, insurance or publishing, then New York is the epicenter of the world for you. What isn't controlled by New York is probably influenced by it. Not as GangsterNomic as Moscow, but close and getting closer.

Las Vegas – This is the fastest growing city in the United States, and is expected to continue a real estate, employment and economic growth curve that will only continue to accelerate.

Kiev, Ukraine – As the capital and largest city in the Ukraine, Kiev is exploding with growth fueled by foreign investors seeking low-wage rates and high growth potential. Though every bit as aggressive as Moscow, Kiev is situated earlier in its growth curve, and therefore possesses the potential to reward sophisticated and well-connected investors with higher rates of return further down the road.

SEVEN GREAT GANGSTERNOMIC LIES

Both the world of crime and business are often built on a foundation of lies. In organized crime, lies are often used to overcome an enemy; in corporate America, deception is most often used to get you to part with $19.95.

Here are some examples:

Free – The word "Free" has been so abused and misused by advertisers, it has become a joke. Statistically speaking, free almost never means free. It usually means you'll receive it if you do "X".

Mail-In Rebate – This is another great joke of modern commerce. Most modern point-of-purchase systems are fully computerized and able to instantly accommodate price changes. If retailers and manufacturers were serious about discounts, they could simply provide you with a price reduction right at the cash register. Instead, they have you mail in a rebate form, knowing full well that 50% of the people will either forget they have one coming, or fail to do anything about not having received it.

Guaranteed – Perhaps one of the most meaningless words in the business lexicon. What is funny about it is that most guarantees have become so meaningless, the very word 'guarantee' seems to have become its own antonym. A situation that is no doubt fueled by all the utterly meaningless extended and lifetime warranties which cover very little or nothing at all when you need them.

Government Insured – This phrase is very common in the world of banking, pensions and insurance; the implication being that if the bottom falls out, you will be covered by the full faith and backing of the U.S. Government. In reality, this type of financial protection is available only in the earliest stages of such a crisis. Once things deteriorate into a large-scale run on the agency by thousands or even millions of claimants, the funding just isn't there to cover everyone.

Price Guarantee – A claim that typically says they will meet or beat any competitor's advertised price. What they usually won't tell you is that this guarantee does not apply to Internet competitors because their prices are simply too low to compete with.

Starting As A Temp May Land You A Full-Time Position – Highly unlikely. But if you do a really great job, are diligent, competent and professional, you may get offered another low-paying, benefit-free, temp job by another employer.

"Virtually" And "Up To" – Both of these usually precede a claim of price or dependability. What they really mean is that you are highly unlikely to see either.

THE MONETIZATION OF DECEPTION

With the possible exception of ruthlessness, there are few things in the worlds of organized crime and corporate America that possess a greater economic value than deception.

It is a quality which permeates all levels of commerce in both the legitimate world as well as organized crime, and is used to add value when there really is none.

Accounting – If recent headlines have revealed anything, it's that the accounting fraud being perpetrated in the supposedly legitimate world of some Fortune 500 companies can dwarf much of the economic wrong-doing being carried out by organized crime.

Manufacturing – The widespread manufacture of bootlegged, cloned and knockoff products is so epidemic that it is even invading industries that were once regarded as relatively safe. One example can be found in the fake pharmaceuticals that are now making their way to some major drug store chains, and are being taken by patients who subsequently pass away because the drugs contained no real medicine.

Marketing – The current level of marketing deception being carried out by organized crime and the corporate world is so blatant and pervasive that it is causing much of the public to disbelieve legitimate marketing claims.

CLOAKING ASSET OWNERSHIP

If criminals and corporations had one goal that they held to be more sacred than all others, it would be the preservation of wealth. Preserving and protecting their wealth is something which makes their very existence possible.

Here are some of the tactics used to cloak asset ownership:

Straw Man Ownership – A straw man is someone of little or no consequence whose name appears on the title to an asset that is really owned or controlled by someone else. The individual is usually paid to pretend they are the owner, and threatened with violence if they reveal they're not.

Corporate Shells – Your ownership of an asset can be concealed by transferring it to a series of corporate shells located offshore. This is a very common technique used to shield an asset from a civil judgement or predatory spouse.

Diminished Value Strategy – Under some circumstances, an asset may be deliberately run-down on the books so that it appears to be worth little if anything. This is often just a crude way of discouraging legal or predatory action when it is not possible to fully cloak its ownership.

Non-Deeded Asset Owner – There are some assets like topless bars and nightclubs which are owned by individuals who have acquired them without ever transferring the deed into their own names. This is usually done by politicians or high-profile businessmen who do not wish to be formally connected to what's perceived to be an unsavory business. The other quite common reason is that the asset is usually given to them as payment for some illegal activity they have been involved in. Formally being declared the owner of an asset so expensive that it could never be acquired by someone in their income bracket would just prove too difficult to explain to the IRS.

SAINT GANGSTER

There comes a point in the career of every gangster, dictator or CEO in which his or her illicit behavior has become so egregious that some sort of public effort needs to be made to repair their image.

This usually occurs about five minutes before the gangster or CEO senses he is about to be indicted. It is at this point that thugs usually start handing out free turkeys, drug cartel members begin building hospitals, and corrupt CEOs start to appear on television giving money away at charity events.

The rational behind all of this is usually based on several desired goals:

Project Benevolence – The idea here to create a public perception of benevolence that is designed to offset much of the negative publicity that has resulted from your previous misdeeds.

Affect Potential Jury Members – This is done to plant positive images and thoughts in the minds of potential future juries that may someday listen to a prosecutor describe every evil deed you've ever committed.

Pave The Way For Your Political Contacts – Here your benevolent and high-profile deeds are designed to make it easier for your political and legal connections to assist you without looking like they have been completely compromised in the process. If they can point to some of the positive things you've done, their advocacy won't look so contrived.

Revise History – By doing this, practitioners of GangsterNomics are often able to practice revisionist history. If they publicly repeat their highly spun version of events often enough, then those details will begin to imprint themselves on the minds of some people as facts.

TV Show Appearances – If you are a major celebrity who has done something inappropriate, it has now become standard operating procedure to appear on a major comedy show and perform a skit designed to trivialize and make light of your current dilemma.

Reinventing yourself under these circumstances isn't about convincing people you are a great person. It's really about trying to humanize you enough to improve your chances with a jury or your fans.

THE ULTIMATE GANGSTERNOMIC HOME

A GangsterNomic home is unlike other homes, because it has to serve several purposes. In addition to providing its owner with shelter and comfort, it must also provide security and the ability to conduct GangsterNomic business in complete and total privacy.

Location – It should be located on a waterfront to maximize its market value. The home should also provide you with multiple egress points so that you are never confined in the event of an emergency.

Architecture – It should have a floor plan which completely separates the living area from the portion of the home you conduct your business in. The home should contain a backup power generator, water supply, and fireproof roof tiles to safeguard it in case of a forest fire.

Security – The home should contain a closed-circuit surveillance system which covers the interior and exterior of the home. You should be able to access your home's video surveillance over the Internet so that you can view them from where ever you are. If the alarm is triggered, your system should notify both your alarm company and yourself by landline and cell phone. Always have a guard dog. They will keep away the smash-and-grab teenagers who like to break in for a quick sixty-second run through the house that lets them grab valuables and get out before the police respond. A tall security fence and gate will keep away solicitors and intruders. Your neighbor's line of sight view into your home windows should always be obscured by fences, walls or landscaping.

Home Office – If you are going to be conducting GangsterNomic business out of your home, then you need a state-of-the-art office. First, you will need two computer systems—one which is never connected to the Internet, and another which is. Needless to say, never share files, disks or CDs between the two. Make certain both computers are fully loaded with state-of-the-art security software and hardware. Conduct your most sensitive business on the non-Internet computer. If you need to do some research online or check your email, do it from the Internet computer. Doing this will minimize the likelihood of your computer being hacked from the outside. Never conduct any banking online, and never allow the banks you do business with to render your bank accounts

Internet-accessible. Both your office landline and cell phones should be scrambled. All your emails should be encrypted and self-destructing. Your office should have a cross cutting shredder which should be used for all paperwork, bills and CDs.

Helipad – If you have serious GangsterNomic money, then a helipad on your estate is absolutely mandatory. Limousines are for millionaires. Helipads are for the GangsterNomic business Gods, whom millionaires aspire to become some day.

THE ULTIMATE GANGSTERNOMIC-MOBILE

People have been conditioned by years of watching movies and television to believe that billionaires and gangsters all drive around in long black stretch limousines, with vanity license plates that spell K.I.S.S .M.Y. C.A.S.H.

In reality, nothing could be further from the truth. It is far more likely that these people will be moving about in very low-key, nondescript gray or neutral colored vehicles.

They are far more apt to be driving around in a very low-profile and unobtrusive minivan or late-model station wagon than in something very flashy. The idea is to cause anyone that may have recognized them to think that it couldn't really be them because they would never be driving something that ordinary.

A major A-List actor was recently asked on late night television why a star of his stature was still commuting by New York subway. He said it is fast and convenient. When asked what he says to people who walk up to ask if it's really him, he said he always does the same thing—he looks them straight in the eye and says,"Now, do you really think if I was him I'd be riding the subway?" At this point they usually nod their heads and walk away disappointed. This is what travelling unobtrusively accomplishes for you.

If they are going to show up at a scheduled movie premiere or serious business meeting then an armored limousine might make sense; but most of the time, slipping in and out without attracting attention is far more important to people at this level.

Just because their vehicles are unobtrusive doesn't mean they are not highly customized. Plain though they may appear, they can still be heavily armored, fitted with the latest communication and GPS tracking devices, and, perhaps most importantly, customized with high-powered turbo-charged engines designed to help them escape from a difficult situation.

Some of these vehicles are so heavily protected that they begin to have more in common with the armored panic rooms seen in upscale homes than they do with ordinary cars.

In areas like Central and South America, the kidnapping and assassination threat level is so off-the-charts that some people are no longer satisfied with Level V vehicle armoring protection (Level V armoring is capable of stopping a NATO 7.62 x 51 armor-piercing round with 147 grains). They are more interested in acquiring vehicle protection against RPG attacks (rocket propelled grenades). To date, the most cost-effective protection against an RPG attack is a driver who makes certain you're never within a mile of one.

REVENGE GANGSTERNOMIC STYLE

One thing that all gangsters, dictators, and corrupt CEOs enjoy more than anything else on this earth is revenge. Not only is it their favorite pastime, but it may also be their most beloved sport.

Sometimes the reasons are petty, and sometimes economic. Whatever the driving force is, you can be certain that they enjoy it. For some of them, a vendetta gives them a purpose in life. It is pursued with a religious fervor that borders on maniacal.

Here are some famous revenge tactics that no one should ever engage in:

Police Informer – This is an old favorite that has ruined more businesses and criminal empires than many of the other revenge tactics combined. What usually happens is that someone who works for you, is married to you, or dates you obtains compromising information. At some point down the line, things take a turn for the worse between the two of you, and in an effort to hurt you they forward this damaging information to law enforcement. GangsterNomic moral of this story? Never confide in anyone.

The Set-Up – This is a great one that is often used by financial advisors, CFOs and business competitors hoping to compromise you. Here you put together an investment opportunity that is sold as a great moneymaker. In reality, it is designed to do little more than implode once your adversary's money is invested. There are few things in life more gratifying than seeing your competitor take a huge loss on a bad investment.

Spousal Seduction – This is extremely popular in the world of organized crime. It falls into the nuclear bomb category of revenge tactics because it's so bad, even criminals refrain from using it until they are sure things have gone well past the point of no return. What they will do is arrange to have the wife or girlfriend of a major adversary seduced and secretly videotaped during the act of infidelity. Whenever possible, they will try to arrange for the paid seducer to be a member of another racial group. A DVD of the infidelity with a date and time stamp on the video will be anonymously mailed to the victim's neighbors, senior management, relatives, in-laws, coworkers, and members of the press. When these DVDs start showing up in mailboxes, even the toughest criminals and CEOs in the world will start smashing furniture and doing cartwheels. They say that the only revenge tactic worse than a videotaped spousal seduction is the one the victim conjures up to get back at you.

False Traitorous Accusation – This revenge tactic is insidious because it is so cancerous. Here's how it works: you obtain some inside information about a major competitor or adversary. Then you send an anonymous letter directly to them stating that this inside information was sent to you by one of his top people. You then name the person, and ask them to refrain from sending you any more information because you are not comfortable with the legal ramifications of all this, and that's why you are responding anonymously. The beauty of this is that the person executing this plan usually selects several of the top people in his adversary's organization to blame. Since the inside information is true and the letter was sent to the victim anonymously, it is a very difficult accusation to defend yourself against. Even if the accused individuals convince their CEO it isn't true, it will be very difficult for him to ever fully trust them again. The passage of time only causes this seed of doubt to grow. When one of the accused people eventually makes a mistake down the road, it will be viewed in a far more sinister light because of this.

False Testimony – This one is extremely popular with incarcerated criminals attempting to reduce their sentences. What they will do is provide false testimony during a trial against a former enemy, in an effort to have their sentence mitigated.

Bad Press – The only thing sweeter than revenge is revenge that is played out in the media. Some people don't just want their enemies destroyed, they want everyone to see it on TV—so they will orchestrate a very complex revenge plot that will include some press coverage of the most embarrassing moments, so it can be see by a film crew that was tipped off in advance.

WAR AND OTHER GREAT GANGSTERNOMIC OPPORTUNITES

There are moments in human psychology when people are almost always willing to pay more than they normally would for a product or service. This occurs during travel, a catastrophe, intoxication, war, and the prospect of an impending sexual encounter.

If you position your product or service to be sold during any of the above situations, then you can charge a significant premium. GangsterNomics is completely devoid of any moral component, and therefore feels no compunction about the context in which a profit is made. If it is legal, then it's fair game. Charging a premium is just an extension of the same logic.

Here are some examples of situations which lend themselves to the charging of significant premiums:

War And Conflict – War is one of the greatest GangsterNomic profit opportunities. There is no other circumstance in the human condition which lends itself more favorably to the suspension of economic reason than war. Whether it is the artificial inflation of gasoline prices or the premium charged for food and water, it all amounts to the same thing—a tendency on the part of manufacturers to exploit a circumstance that often has little or no impact on their business model.

Travel – This is another great human predisposition—the tendency to accept higher prices when travelling—as if being sold at an airport or gas station is any justification at all for charging 30% more than usual. This psychological predisposition goes back over a century ago, to a time when food and water became more scarce as you traveled further from home. Now it is just something that is engrained in our economic psychology, and thus taken for granted.

Catastrophe – Like wars, catastrophes create a heightened opportunity for economic gain. The emotional vortex catastrophes create often diminishes people's ability to object to the premiums they are being charged. Whether it's insurance companies that refuse to pay a substantial portion of a homeowner's claim, or charging ten percent more for the plywood you need to board up your windows before a hurricane arrives, the end result is usually the same. Catastrophes generate far more profit than cost for most companies.

Intoxication – Drinking not only loosens the purse strings, but it also diminishes one's ability to object to an inflated price. Whether it's a casino that gets you tipsy enough to lose more money at their blackjack table, or a nightclub that charges you ten dollars for a glass of liquor the size of a thumbnail, the net result is a higher profit margin.

Impending Sexual Encounter – With the possible exception of having a gun placed against one's temple, nothing encourages people to spend money like the prospect of an impending sexual encounter. Men will spend $100 on a steak dinner they could have made at home for eight bucks. Women will spend five thousand dollars to have two $5 silicone bags inserted into their chests. It's almost as though one's libido completely overrides the portion of one's brain that governs economic reason.

Health – This is the mother of all GangsterNomic opportunities. Nothing encourages people to spend money like the prospect of dying if they don't. Hospitals have elevated the art of overcharging to something approaching the sacrosanct. Think about the significance of this for a moment—hospitals now routinely charge more money than most people accumulate throughout their entire lives for just a few hours of their time on the operating table. With this kind of historically unprecedented greed, it's only a matter of time before hospital-based debt becomes so enormous that the cost of an operation for someone with no insurance will be passed down from generation to generation like 100-year mortgages in Japan.

If you review some of the wealthiest entities in the world like insurance companies, arms manufacturers, hospital chains, pharmaceuticals and HMOs, you will find that their business models are built around the economic exploitation of pain, misery and catastrophe. If anything, their success in these areas highlights how important it is to remove any and all compassion or humanity from each and every business decision one makes. An argument can even be made that introducing compassion into business drives down profit almost as aggressively as incompetence.

THE DEVIL'S OWN OCCUPATION

Most people are under the mistaken impression that the sale of narcotics or computer chips are the most profitable businesses in the world. They're not even close. The most profitable industry on earth is the arms business.

Just to give you a sense of scale, a major defense contractor was recently awarded a $200 billion contract to manufacture the Joint Strike Fighter for the Air Force, Navy and Marines. That's billion with a "b", and it is just one contract for one company. There are many more defense contractors and arms dealers around the world generating revenues so enormous that the money being paid for their goods and services can literally affect the GNP of some of the nations doing business with them.

As GangsterNomic businesses go, the arms business is at the top of the food chain. Not only is it far more ruthless than drug dealing, it also possesses a business model that is self-perpetuating.

Arms dealers are famous for selling weapons to both sides of a conflict. The beauty of this business model is that selling more weapons to one side guarantees that their adversary will have to increase their weapons purchases just to survive.

Another highly lucrative aspect of the arms industry is that the cost of maintaining a weapon system over time can be almost as expensive as purchasing it. It means that many weapon system purchases can continue to generate a maintenance revenue stream years after they're purchased.

If one were to quantify the degree of ruthlessness endemic to various industries with a scale of one to ten, it's clear the arms business would leap off the chart. The medical profession may allow you to die if you can't afford their services, but the arms industry will allow you to wipe out an entire city if you've got the cash.

THE MINISTRY OF GANGSTERNOMICS

If there is such a thing as the anti-spiritual epicenter of GangsterNomics, then it must reside on Wall Street. It has become the modern day economic equivalent of Sodom & Gomorrah. An electronic Ministry of GangsterNomics that draws evil and corruption, the way Lourdes attracts the sick and disabled. There is no other place on earth where more time, money and energy are poured into relieving other people of their wealth than Wall Street.

For those who thought that the recent economic reforms would have cleaned matters up, think again. There are a number of legislative packages being considered or introduced by people hoping to ease or eliminate the heightened corporate governance safeguards that were enacted recently.

REVERSING AMERICAN JOB LOSSES

Left unchecked, the high-speed exodus of American jobs overseas will eventually cripple our economy, and render this country very disadvantaged when dealing with other nations. Ideally the problem would be addressed at the policy level, but as this appears unlikely in the near future, I would like to propose a more innovative option.

I believe that one way to reduce the flight of American jobs to low-wage nations, as well as retrieve many of the jobs we have already lost, is to modify our intellectual property laws with a new two-tier patent system.

A Tier 1 Patent would provide the same level and duration of patent protection for new technology, business models, or products that our existing intellectual property laws currently make available.

A Tier 2 Patent would offer greater protection to holders of patents by tripling the duration of the Tier 1 patent life in exchange for legally agreeing to exclusively manufacture your product in the United States for the length of the patent. The Tier 2 Patent law would also possess an "Existing Jobs Repatriation" clause, which stated that if you were 1) currently in possession of a conventional patent that was due to expire, and 2) were willing to immediately relocate all your foreign plants and jobs back to the United States, then you would qualify for a Tier 2 Patent.

Here's the theory: if you want to manufacture overseas, then apply for a conventional Tier 1 Patent. You may save some money on labor costs in the short term, but if you obtain a Tier 2 Patent on your new product or business model, then it will last three times longer than a Tier 1 patent, which will provide you with many more decades of profit and exclusivity. If your accountants do a quick analysis, they'll find that the enormous profit you will generate by having a patent that lasts three times longer will dramatically exceed any savings you may have realized by using low-wage overseas labor during the life of your much shorter Tier 1 patent.

If you currently manufacture or have jobs overseas under the protection of a pre-existing patent, then you could dramatically increase the length of that patent by agreeing to bring your jobs back to the U.S. in exchange for a Tier 2 Patent under the "Existing Jobs Repatriation" provision.

The economic advantages America would realize in terms of jobs and tax revenue by creating this new two-tier patent system would be tremendous. Patent applicants would still have the option to manufacture or hire people where ever they wanted to under Tier 1. But if they would like to generate much more revenue over a much greater time period, they will have the option of doing that by agreeing to hire U.S. workers and manufacturing their product in America for the life of the Tier 2 patent.

TRUE LIES IN THE MEDIA

You will find that much of what has been revealed to you in this book will be proven true in a really interesting way. First, you and your family will begin to personally experience much of what has been forecast here in the coming years. Secondly, the media will try to counter what people are experiencing with reports designed to convince them that the overall picture is really much better than any geographically isolated pocket of economic adversity may indicate. Ignore these stories completely, for they are based on fabricated statistics that bear no reality to the truth. As the economic meltdown accelerates, you will see a disturbing disconnect between what's being told to you by the media and what you see all around you. When things reach this level, you'll know that the economy is in serious trouble, because these stories are designed to prevent outright panic. As a television producer I have the inside information it takes to determine which reporters, members of the media, and talk show hosts you should listen to when things begin to get rough. If you are interested in honesty, credibility and integrity, then the following list of reporters can only be described as the very best of the best. We have given each of them a "GangsterNomic Media Honesty Rating" between 1 and 10. The higher the number, the more integrity we feel they and their programs possess. In my opinion, anyone with a GangsterNomic Media Honesty Rating below 5 should be stuffed into a clown suit and forced to work on a pig farm for a year before they're allowed to get back on the air to tell more lies to hard-working people.

Bill O'Reilly, *The O'Reilly Factor,* **FOX News** – If someone were to invent a combination chainsaw and flame-thrower that sprays out the truth at the same time as it dismembers liars, frauds and hypocrites, then I'm sure they would have to consult with Bill first. I have never seen anyone who enjoys annihilating scumbags more than he does. There is nothing more entertaining than watching some politician, celebrity or businessman on Bill's show at the precise moment he catches them in a lie. It's like seeing a close up of one of Mike Tyson's opponents just before his jaw is shattered and he gets sent home to mama in a wheelbarrow. That is how ferociously aggressive Bill is when it comes to pursuing the truth. **GangsterNomic Media Honesty Rating: 9.4**

Chris Matthews, *Hardball,* **MSNBC** – What I like about Chris is that not only is he brilliant, but he speaks so quickly that most of the lying hacks he has on his show don't have time to construct a good lie. You can see their crooked eyeballs start to rotate in opposing directions as they labor to come up with an answer to a question he asked seven sentences earlier. His speed-interview technique is like a "truth blitzkrieg" that leaves his lying guests sitting naked in a cornfield wondering what the hell just happened. **GangsterNomic Media Honesty Rating: 9.2**

Donny Deutsch, *The Big Idea,* **CNBC** – Donny is both a great businessman and an advertising genius who can smell a lie three time zones away. His guests, business partners and friends respect him because he is both intelligent and gracious. Best of all, he's rich enough not to have to lie. **GangsterNomic Media Honesty Rating: 8.9**

Greta Van Susteren, *On The Record,* **Fox News** – Greta is as sharp as they come, and extremely well respected for her astute legal analysis of stories and situations. **GangsterNomic Media Honesty Rating: 8.8**

Larry King, *Larry King Live,* **CNN** – Larry King possesses something that few other reporters and news agencies can match—he has access to high-level VIPs and dignitaries who respect and trust him enough to come on his show when they are unwilling to appear anywhere else. That's the kind of access that makes him both unique and newsworthy. **GangsterNomic Media Honesty Rating: 9.0**

Lou Dobbs, *Lou Dobbs Tonight,* **CNN** – Lou Dobbs is on almost every night fighting to bring attention to the way America's economy is being dismantled by foreign interests all across the globe. The great thing about Lou is that he never backs down or accepts ridiculous corporate spin. More importantly, he has been fighting for the little guy long before it was P.C. to do so. Lou is a good man. **GangsterNomic Media Honesty Rating: 9.3**

Matt Drudge, *The Drudge Report* **, Drudgereport.com** – What's interesting about Matt is how jealous mainstream reporters and news agencies are of him. They practically have a stroke every time he breaks a news story ahead of them. This is one guy with a website that routinely scoops billion-dollar news agencies that are going insane trying to figure out how he does it. I love the way so many

223

mainstream reporters publicly attack Matt, while they privately check his website three times a day for stories they can steal. Matt Drudge's news aggregating website is the future paradigm of reporting, and most mainstream reporters secretly begrudge him for it. **GangsterNomic Media Honesty Rating: 9.1**

Matt Lauer, *The Today Show*, NBC – Everyone who knows Matt will tell you the same thing—he possesses the perfect combination of grace, charm and intelligence needed to contend with the endless parade of half-witted, barely sober celebrities that sit across from him. He is tenacious and honest, and that is something that everyone respects about him. **GangsterNomic Media Honesty Rating: 8.8**

Mike Wallace, *60 Minutes*, CBS – Mike has ended the career of more corrupt politicians, businessmen and crazy whacked-out celebrities than any ten reporters I can think of. Insiders joke that fire escape ladders were invented for guys who see Mike coming through the front door to interview them. I'm convinced that *60 Minutes* and reporters like Mike Wallace have literally made the United States a safer and better country to live in. **GangsterNomic Media Honesty Rating: 9.7**

Oprah Winfrey, *The Oprah Winfrey Show* – Oprah's soul, voice and behavior all resonate with honesty. She excels at putting a human face on many of the problems which face our society, and that's one of the many reasons viewers love her. You almost get the impression that God put her on this planet to compensate us for much of the evil which roams the earth so freely. **GangsterNomic Media Honesty Rating: 9.2**

The people I have listed above are the most honest in the business, but what's really important is that you not rely exclusively on the media for all your information. Build up your own network of friends and business associates all across the country, and make it a point to exchange information with them as often as possible. If you combine what you are told by the media with the information you receive from trusted contacts, then you will have a more accurate picture of what's really occurring.

POST-APOCALYPTIC GANGSTERNOMIC BUSINESS STRATEGY

The problem with unbridled commercial ruthlessness is that it just creates more ruthlessness. It is a vicious and self-perpetuating phenomenon that will only escalate until their goal of seizing your job, home, business and savings is realized.

If you know that much, then you have to conclude that the level of GangsterNomics out there will only intensity, which is going to make things even more difficult.

If you are a practitioner of GangsterNomics, you will have an increased chance to succeed. If not, then it is very likely you're just going to struggle.

I am going to provide you with some options you should consider when mapping out your long-term goals and strategies. What follows are some GangsterNomic suggestions and strategies designed to improve your financial ability to withstand, endure and survive the "greed storm" that is coming:

Homes – If you live in a single family home, then try to cash out and purchase a larger two, three or even four-family home. When the housing bubble bursts, there will be countless people who can no longer afford their mortgages, but can still afford to rent. When that happens, you want to be a landlord and not a homeowner because of the income streams the other units in your building will provide you.

Banking – If you do all your banking with one bank, then you should consider withdrawing two-thirds of your money and depositing it into two other banks. This way, your assets will be divided between three bank institutions. If one of them fails, you will still have access to at least two-thirds of your assets. The FDIC Guarantee you see posted on the doors of most banks will probably fail to cover the deposits in your bank if there is a major and protracted problem with the economy. If you are of significant means and you have the wherewithal, you should consider depositing some of your assets in a Swiss bank. Unlike American Banks, many Swiss banks do not loan out the money they have in their accounts. They actually make their money by charging fees, not issuing loans. That means the money you put into a bank like that will probably still be there when things take a turn for the worse.

Stop Reading So Much Of The Sports Page – Take ninety percent of the time and effort you spend discussing sports, reading the sports page, and watching sports on television and devote it to studying money and business opportunities. Nothing your favorite sports team will ever do is going to enhance the quality of your life or put more money in your bank account. Being a sports enthusiast over the age of eighteen is fine; just try to keep it in perspective. Focus on those things which will make you money and improve your family's quality of life.

Globalize Your Business – If you are an independent businessman who is struggling to make ends meet in the U.S., then start aggressively looking for options overseas.

Ignore Half Of The Reports You're About To See – As things begin to economically deteriorate, you will see many government reports designed to convince you that things are really much better than they are. Ignore most of that nonsense, and remember that things are rarely as good or as bad as they're portrayed.

Stay Out Of The Stock Market – The stock market is like Las Vegas. Most of the people who go there claim to have made a profit, but rarely ever do. There is very little statistical difference between selecting stocks and gambling in a casino.

Never Confuse Religion With Business – If people got a glimpse of how some major religious organizations run the business side of their affairs, they'd run straight to the police. Consequently, most of these religious organizations are in no position to judge or tell you what the proper way to conduct business is. As long as what you're doing is completely legal, then you're okay. Beyond that, everything else is subjectively colored by the judgmental biases of individual perspectives.

Train Your Children To Be More Financially Sophisticated Than You Are – Soccer on the weekends is great. Playing video games after they've completed their homework is fine. But if you really want to make them strong and independent when they're your age, spend a little time with them each week to sharpen their business skills. Teach them to aspire to be a business owner some day. Instill in them a love of information, and a desire to learn from the success of others. I'm not talking about turning them into little yuppie Nazis whose lives revolve around materialism. I'm talking about opening their minds to the way the world really works; instilling within them a desire to own a sports team rather than just chase a basketball up and down the court.

Embrace Future Economic Downturns – Start viewing all economic problems as opportunities. Whenever things take a turn for the worse, there are always a hundred people complaining and three folks who have figured out how to make money off the problem. Become one of those three people.

Professional Paranoia – If you are a business owner, adopt a level of professional paranoia designed to heighten your awareness of all the efforts being made to compromise or seize your business. Stop worrying about what your competitors are doing to compete with you, and start worrying about all the secretive efforts being made to take everything you own outright.

News Sources – Make it a point to obtain more of your news from uncensored, unbiased, high-tech Internet-based sources. It is also very important to monitor international news sources to obtain a differing world viewpoint.

Competitive Extermination – Adjust your business mindset so that you stop viewing competition as something that occurs between rivals pursuing the same goal, and start viewing it as something your rival is doing to drive you into extinction. If you understand that, you are better equipped to undermine his economic efforts and defeat them.

FIND THE ECONOMIC ZEN IN THAT
WHICH CONFRONTS YOU

Remember you weren't placed on this earth just to make money. Hopefully you realize you were placed here to fulfill some higher purpose. Keep that perspective in mind when you are navigating the economic path that makes sense for you.

SUMMARY

As organized crime and the legitimate world of multinational corporations compete for the same limited resources, it is creating pressure on both groups to adopt the latest and most successful business models and technology. As one group achieves a success that becomes visible to the other, it creates a tremendous incentive to modify and adopt that approach for one's own benefit. The result of this unholy convergence is a ruthless and diabolical gray area of activity called GangsterNomics. It is a new business paradigm that is becoming so pervasive it is affecting our entire society, and that is going to make life in the coming years very interesting.

COMING SOON

Watch for **GangsterZilla**™. It's the next book from writer, producer John Surowy. **GangsterZilla**™ is an inside look at the next generation of super gangsters engaging in criminal activity clever enough to affect the United State's Gross National Product.

HOLLYWOODISCALLING.COM

Now you can purchase live phone calls and email video greeting cards from over 80 celebrities and athletes. Whether you'd like to have a celebrity make a live birthday call to a friend's cell phone or you're interested in having a celebrity make a live telephonic personal appearance at your next fundraiser, HollywoodIsCalling.com is the company for you.

DANGER ISLAND

For the first time in history a next generation reality television show will take you to a place where even the Gods themselves fear to tread. We're going to place twelve real life convicted felons (six men and six women) on a deserted tropical island and have them compete for one million dollars ($1,000,000 U.S.) prize that will be given to the victim of the winner's last crime. All their lives these felons have behaved like predators as they victimized innocent men and women. Now they'll become the prey as they compete in extraordinary physical and psychological contests designed to let them know what it feels like to be stalked through the jungle.

Professional Manhunters will be brought in from all over the world to try and catch the felons before they are able to complete each episode's contest. If they complete the contest before they are caught then they move onto the next round... but if they're caught then they're removed from the show. Some episodes will include a group of actual crime victims voting one criminal off the island. Danger Island will be the first show in entertainment history to take actual criminals, turn the tables on them, and show them what it feels like to become the hunted. To learn more about "Danger Island" visit www.DangerIsland.TV

235

GODFATHER COURT

For those of you who thought reality television couldn't possibly get any more exciting we're going to produce a next generation reality comedy show called "Godfather Court" in which real people litigate real cases in front of a panel of judges comprised of ex-criminals as well as actors who've played gangsters in the movies.

Then just when you thought it couldn't get any better we make things even more interesting. In Godfather Court the normal rule of law will not apply because we're going to encourage people to lie as they present their cases. In fact, whether you win your case or not may depend entirely on how convincing and pathologically gifted you are as a liar. While real courtroom lawyers and litigants pretend to tell the truth to win their cases we'll tolerate no such nonsense here. The better you lie the more apt you are to win your case. Everybody knows that our real judicial system is corrupt beyond measure. Why bother hiding it anymore? Why not make an entertaining and comedic reality show out of it? So, in keeping with that spirit we're going to bring in real ex-criminals as well as actors who've played gangsters on the screen and empower them to dispense some of the most entertaining and comedic justice viewers have ever seen. To learn more about Godfather Court visit www.Godfathercourt.com

SAVANT EDITING SERVICES

Professional editing and proofreading consultation designed to accommodate your schedule and budget.

As a freelance editor, I possess a wealth of experience spanning a decade, editing a wide variety of documents including manuscripts, book proposals, journal articles, scientific and technical manuals, as well as the book you see this advertisement in.

To discuss how we can make your great project even better, contact me at: editingsavant@hotmail.com

www.ingramcontent.com/pod-product-compliance
Lightning Source LLC
Chambersburg PA
CBHW071420090426
42737CB00011B/1520